Reinventing Your Rainbow

A Spiritual Journey of Leaving the Dark Shadows of Satan's Bondage to Discover the Magnificent Colorful Rainbow That God Holds for Your Life

Tracie W. Miles

PublishAmerica
Baltimore

First printing

All definitions are from Miriam-Webster Online (www.webster.com).

Softcover 1-4241-5016-7
PAperback 978-1-4512-5107-4
PUBLISHED BY PUBLISHAMERICA, LLLP
www.publishamerica.com
Baltimore

Printed in the United States of America

To my wonderful husband, Michael—
You are truly my soul mate. I have always loved you and always will. Thank you for your support and encouragement, but mostly for believing in me.

To my three children,
Morgan, Kaitlyn, and Michael—
You are more precious to me than you will ever know. You bring joy to my life that can only be compared to the joy that I have through Christ. May you always put Christ first in your lives, and have an abundance of rainbows in your hearts.

Table of Contents

INTRODUCTION

Life is made up of many colors. As a tiny new infant we are pure, symbolized by the color white. Although we are all sinners at birth, we have yet to willfully commit any sins. But as we grow, our life takes on many colors—yellow for happy times, red for times of anger, blue when we are sad, or black when we are in the midst of sin, trials and suffering or even lost in the wilderness away from God. Life is a rainbow filled with happy colors and sad colors, but all of these vibrant colors come together to make us a unique and whole individual.

For many years, my heart's rainbow was missing. Although I had a wonderful life, my rainbow was overshadowed by a dark and sinister cloud that had covered me when I was just a teenager and had kept my heart and mind captive for many years. This cloud was a barrier to all the beautiful colors of life that wanted to saturate my missing rainbow.

The cloud was sin. I had sinned, and I was living with the belief that God could never forgive me for what I had done. He could never look past it, never see me as His precious child, and certainly never forget. I truly believed to the depths of my soul that I had committed the unpardonable sin, and that my slate in heaven was eternally scarred. But now I know that I am forgiven, thanks to God's ultimate saving grace, mercy and love for each of His precious children. God's forgiveness and mercy is complete and able to overpower anything that the devil brings our way. However, sadly enough, I wasted many years of my life believing Satan's lie—the lie that God could never forgive me or love me.

I would imagine that you too have committed sins that are painful to remember and bring sadness to your heart. Maybe these sins have become scary skeletons in your closet of life, but take heart in knowing that every individual has at least one or two skeletons in their closet that they hope will never surface. These skeletons could be sins that you have tried to forget and secretly feel that God could never forgive you for. They may be sins in which you have asked forgiveness from God and tried to forget. Alternately, you may have asked for forgiveness, but just can't seem to forgive yourself, and as a result you spend year after year carrying that pain inside your heart, allowing yourself to be held hostage by sin, and giving the devil a stronghold on your life. Friends, Jesus came to set the captives free. You can be set free from the bondage of sin, the chains of shame, and the emotional torture of guilt.

The chapters of this book will carry you through my personal journey of adolescence, bad decisions, fear, pain, regret, and remorse. But most importantly, it is a beautiful journey of forgiveness, restoration, renewed hope, and my quest to reinvent my heart, and myself, which led to the creation of a vibrant rainbow in my life through the compassion and love of my Savior, Jesus. It is a journey that allowed me to become the woman which God had destined for me to become. Lastly, it is a journey that is a shining example of how God is always in control of the ride that life takes us on, even when we think we are holding the steering wheel.

Dear friend, I pray that through the pages of this book you will begin your own personal journey and find restoration and renewal and joy. I pray that you will come to understand, accept and believe that God will forgive you for any sin as soon as you ask Him for forgiveness. Delayed forgiveness is merely a by-product of our delay to ask for it. That delayed forgiveness results in delayed joy.

My prayer is that for the first time in many years, you can allow yourself to have the peace and abundant joy that you deserve and that the God of creation desires for your life.

So hold on tight, and get ready for a journey to discover your rainbow.

ONE
What Is the Rainbow of Life?

In Genesis 9:13-14, God tell us, *"I have set my rainbow in the clouds, and it will be the sign of the covenant between me and the earth. Whenever I bring clouds over the earth and the rainbow appears in the clouds, I will remember my covenant between me and you and all living creatures of every kind."*

There are only a few people who can say they have never seen a rainbow. Rainbows bless us with their beauty more frequently than we realize, not only in the sky, but in the spray of a water hose, a glass reflection on the ceiling, or a shimmer on a mirror. The sight of a rainbow always draws attention to all who can see it and conjures up feelings of beauty, hope and happiness.

In fact, even Dorothy from *The Wizard of Oz* yearned for a rainbow. But what was it about the rainbow that made Dorothy sing? She yearned for what she thought was impossible here on earth— love, peace and happiness; she was sure those things could only be found over the rainbow. Her Oz counterparts hoped to find a renewed heart, a badge of courage, and true wisdom. The moral of that movie was to signify that those things were Dorothy's own deepest desires for herself and her life, which is why she dreamed so vividly about trying to reach the magnificent Land of Oz, which supposedly held those coveted treasures. She wanted to create a rainbow of her own that would provide her the hope, peace, happiness, and wisdom that she felt would lead to a more fulfilling life. What Dorothy didn't realize was that the rainbow is merely a symbol for the deepest desires of our hearts, but the Creator of the rainbow is the only way to true peace, fulfillment and joy.

The rainbow was a gift from God to His people, a promise of His love for His people. But what many people do not consider is that a rainbow can also be viewed as a metaphor for our entire lives.

Let's break down the actual definition of the word "rainbow" to help give you more insight into God's creation. The word "rainbow" can be interpreted in several different ways:

(a) An arc of spectral colors, usually identified as red, orange, yellow, green, blue, indigo, and violet, that appears in the sky opposite the sun as a result of the refractive dispersion of sunlight in drops of rain or mist; a graded display of colors.

(b) An illusory hope; chasing the rainbow

(c) A diverse assortment or collection.

You can apply these definitions to the normal progression of life, with all of life's ups and downs, twists and turns. If you consider definition (a), each color can signify a certain time or experience in our life. Although these are the primary colors in a rainbow, they are most definitely not the only colors. We all learned the "ROYGBIV" abbreviation in elementary school to help us remember the colors and the sequence of colors in a rainbow, but in reality there could be thousands of different colors that the human eye just can't see.

When gazing upon a rainbow, it is difficult to distinguish where one color ends and the other begins, since all of the colors gradually merge into one another. As the colors merge together, new colors are created. For example, when mixed together, red and white become pink; blue and yellow make green; red and blue make purple. In addition, each color has infinite shades and varying levels of color intensity.

Take a moment to visualize what an artist's palette looks like. In the beginning, before an artist begins to work, all of the colors are just small globs of paint, each neatly placed on the palette. Once the artist begins spreading the paintbrush across the paint to form his masterpiece, the colors get mixed together, and new colors and shades are created. Apply this concept to your life and visualize God being the artist. We all have the standard colors in our rainbow of life, but as we proceed through life, our colors get mixed together, new colors form, and our life becomes a masterpiece of the mixture of all the colors.

As already mentioned, each experience, or color of life, does not have a definitive start and end date. But as each color, a.k.a. experience, merges into one another, we mature, grow and learn. It is those learning experiences that transition us into the next phase of our life. In actuality, we all spend our entire lives chasing after our rainbows, searching for hope —definition (b)—even if we don't realize it. We all want what is best for us, our lives, and our families, and as a result we spend our lives dealing with all the diverse assortments and collections of colors— definition (c)—that are flooding our lives while trying to pursue the perfect rainbow.

Rain and Sunshine Illuminate Our Lives

Now let's consider another important aspect of what it takes for a rainbow to form and compare that to our own lives. In order for a rainbow to be present, there must be the presence of rain and sunshine. In our lives we have times of rain, and we have times of sunshine. Although we all secretly desire that there would never be any rain, or sadness, in our lives, it is a combination of these sad and happy experiences that create our rainbows of life. You cannot have a rainbow without a combination of rain and sunshine.

I want to take a moment to break down all the internal details of a rainbow so you can truly understand the rainbow analogy before delving into the remaining chapters of this book. Did you know that the vividness of colors in a rainbow depends on the size of the raindrops? Large raindrops result in bright rainbows with well-defined colors; small droplets produce rainbows of overlapping colors that appear nearly white. Water droplets are always a mixture of sizes and shapes. Similarly, our life is made up of large raindrops, which represent significant trials, and tiny raindrops, which represent small, everyday trials. Our raindrops can be filled with lovely colors, such as the birth of our children, success in a job, a marriage, a once-in-a-lifetime vacation, or a special memory. But our raindrops can also be black and dreary, such as the loss of a loved one, abortion, divorce, serious illness or sin. It is a combination of all of these raindrops of life that water our lives and help us grow into the person that we are today.

We are not born with character; instead God gives us the opportunity to develop it. An individual's unique character is grown over time, as a result of all of the colors that make up our rainbows. Although we cannot always control the circumstances that are taking place in our lives, good or bad, it is our choice to determine how those circumstances will affect our character, and what colors we will allow those raindrops to bring to our rainbow.

The "bow" part of the word rainbow describes the fact that the rainbow is a group of nearly circular arcs of color which all have a common center. As a result of all these facets I have mentioned, the rainbow can truly be viewed as a symbol of our lives. A myriad of colors fading in and out, but regardless of circumstances, all of the colors, bright or dreary, stay hovered around one central core.

For all Christians, God is our central core. He should be the center of our rainbow of life. When God is not the center, the colors of our rainbow will be dull and faded, maybe even missing in action.

One last thing I want you to consider. When we view a rainbow, we see an arc, but are you aware that you just can't see the whole picture? The only reason that the human eye sees an arc instead of a full circle is because the earth blocks our view. Rainbows are actually a full circle! And inside this circle of light, the sky is brighter than on the outside. The contrast of light inside the arc is actually brighter than the sky outside the arc. White is considered a color, but it is actually a mixture of all the colors of light. All of the colors bouncing off the sky at the exact same time display the color of white light. The color white symbolizes purity. Purity symbolizes our Lord Jesus Christ.

Purity means "the condition of being pure; freedom from sin or guilt; innocence, chastity; lacking of knowledge or evil" (*Webster's Dictionary*). If God is the center of our life, then our life will be fully enclosed around Him, and the center of our lives will be focused on the purity of righteousness. Isaiah 1:18 says, *"Come now, let us reason together, says the Lord. Though your sins are like scarlet, they shall be as white as snow; though they are red as crimson, they shall be like wool."*

The sequence of the color spectrum is such that red is the outer color of the rainbow. It is the color farthest from the center, or area of purity. Red signifies sin. Isaiah 1:18 "...*though they are red as crimson, they shall be like wool.*" The bottom color of a rainbow is violet, also known as purple or indigo. This is the color closest to the center area of purity, the ring of color that surrounds the center of the rainbow and is closest to the earth. The color indigo signifies royalty, as often seen in the movies on kings who parade around their kingdoms wearing long velvet robes of elegant indigo. Royalty means "one that has power; one that can bring justice on others." Jesus is the one and only true king, the king of all kings, and He is our royalty. He is the one and only holy being that can bring justice on us, but who suffered injustice on our behalf so that we could have eternal life.

Despite your efforts for happiness and peace, maybe that perfect rainbow continues to seem far away in the distance. Maybe it seems so far away that you can't see it with even the brightest sunlight. Maybe your rainbow is missing too, because you have sins in your past that are clouding your view and hindering you from pursuing the abundant joy that God desires for you. Have confidence in knowing that the Lord our God can and will remove those clouds, if only you allow Him to. It's up to you to give it up to Him.

A rainbow is one of the most magnificent displays of nature on this earth. Each time I see a rainbow, large or small, vivid or faint, I instantly feel engulfed by the love of Jesus. I feel the urge to immediately praise Him for not only allowing me to see this spectacular wonder of creation once again, but for the promise of His love that it provides.

In Genesis 9:13-14, God tells us, *"I have set my rainbow in the clouds, and it will be the sign of the covenant between me and the earth. Whenever I bring clouds over the earth and the rainbow appears in the clouds, I will remember my covenant between me and you and all living creatures of every kind."*

Please don't take this verse too lightly. The rainbow is not merely a promise that God will never flood the earth again. It is a promise of His overwhelming love. It is a promise that we can actually see with our human eyes, and a promise which resounds every time a rainbow washes against the horizon.

The colors of a rainbow were not tossed into the sky as an afterthought when the flood was over. They were divinely determined by God and divinely placed in a specific order to symbolize not only God's love, but also the meaning of life.

The beauty of your rainbow is in your hands. Throughout your life, the colors of your rainbow will fade in and out, and you will always be merging from one color to another. But regardless of your circumstances, in order for the colors to be vibrant and alive, God must remain as the pure and holy center of your rainbow. The stories outlined in this book will not only show you how I achieved my rainbow, but will hopefully be the light you have been looking for to brighten up your journey as you set out to discover the colors of your rainbow that are waiting to burst forth and bring joy and happiness to the core of your soul.

TWO
The Building of the Ark

Genesis 6:9: *"Noah was a righteous man, blameless among the people of his time, and he walked with God."*

Shades of Green

The color green is a beautiful color. When I think of shades of green, many things come to mind, such as shining emeralds, beautiful foliage in the spring and summer, sparkling Christmas trees, and mint chocolate ice cream. But green can also be defined as being young, immature, youthful, vigorous, brand new, and lacking training or experience. At some point in our lives, we have probably all been called "a little green," especially when taking on new challenges such as beginning college or starting a new job or career. There are always people more experienced and more seasoned. But when we are young, we live in the green years—so full of life and energy, with an excitement for everything new…but also out of touch with the real world. As children, we are like sponges in the pool of life, hungry to learn about knowledge and life, and we regress to taking on the role of the sponge each time we start a new journey at any age as we strive to grow, learn and mature.

I was born to wonderful parents in 1967, as a very healthy ten-pound baby girl. From that moment on, God blessed me with a wonderful life, from infancy to adulthood, and growing up in the

1970s and '80s was an adventure, especially considering that both of those decades were fashion disasters. But my dear mother stayed faithful in her pursuit to ban me from wearing "parachute pants" and mini-skirts with leggings as much as possible.

My father's job occasionally moved us around the Southeast, but my family finally settled down when I was in the fourth grade, in the small town of Rome, Georgia. My elementary and middle school years were filled with fond memories as I blossomed into a young lady, and my high school years flew by as I gradually learned the trials and adventures of growing up.

I was raised in a Christian home with loving parents and a wonderful sister and brother, but eventually my parents' marriage experienced unexpected difficulties, although both of my parents were Christians. Unfortunately, as we all know, Christianity is not the prevention method for divorce. The statistics tell us that an astonishing 50% of Christian marriages end in divorce. But it leads me to wonder if these marriages in crisis are truly Christian marriages or if they are just a product of two Christians who got married. There is a big difference.

I recall in my childhood countless times listening to my parents argue about a variety of things, and although I don't remember the topics, it was always saddening to listen to heated arguments by people who were supposed to love each other. After months, maybe years, of a serious lack of marital bliss in our household, my parents finally made the decision to separate and stayed separated for seven years before finalizing their divorce.

Unlike some people, I rarely remember the intricate details of all the positive or negative occurrences of my childhood. In fact, my mother often gets very frustrated when my siblings and I can't remember a special family vacation or a visit to a significant landmark that they had taken us to so that we could have wonderful childhood memories to treasure. But fortunately for my mother, my brother claims he can remember things from when he was two years old; being that I can hardly remember what I did last year, I often find myself skeptical of people who make such claims! The downside of my brother's miraculous memory is that a lot of his memories seem to include times when I supposedly "tortured" him during his childhood, as big brothers and sisters too often do to younger siblings. I stand firm in my adamant dispute of any claims of those incidences, especially the one claiming that I tried to put his head in the toilet and another time that I supposedly tied him to the large oak tree in the front yard until my parents arrived home and rescued him.

Shades of Baby Blue

There is one vivid memory that I can conjure up, which is when my father left home. This is the time of my life when I moved out of the green era and into the blue. The word "blue" automatically instills thoughts of depression and gloominess, and sometimes that is the case. But at that time, I was just too young to know what being blue really meant. I really didn't know how to process my feelings and what to think. The divorce was a traumatic event for me at the tender age of 15, and also for my 13-year-old sister and nine-year-old brother, but mainly for my parents. Months and sometimes years of anguish lead up to a divorce, it is not something done on a whim. Regardless, I felt devastated and abandoned when my dad left home.

On the surface, we were a happy family. We looked great in the church pictorial directory. We lived in a beautiful suburban home with a big yard and thick oak trees, and pastures behind the house full of cows and horses. We spent our days playing with the neighborhood kids; staying out after dark to catch fireflies; raking the fall leaves in the front yard and forming them into a house of our own, complete with rooms, hallways and doorways; riding bicycles for hours without a care in the world; building snowmen and being pulled on our sleds behind the neighbor's pickup truck; wonderful holidays blessed with family gatherings and too many presents; jumping on the trampoline with friends; attending church every Sunday, and going on youth group retreats. All the things that would symbolize the all-American family and that a happy child in a Christian home would experience, but still there were rain clouds forming.

Since I was still in high school when my parents went through their separation, I was too young to know or understand all of the details, and honestly I didn't want to know. I only knew that I didn't like what was happening, and it was not fair. The divorce affected each family member in different ways, and our hurts would surface unexpectedly at different times and in various situations throughout our life. For example, one year my sister was elected to homecoming court at our high school. After the announcement of her accomplishment was made over the loud speaker at the school, I later found her in the hallway weeping, only to find out that she was afraid that she wouldn't be able to have her daddy walk her onto the football field during the homecoming ceremony, which was the custom. This is another one of those moments I'll never forget despite my forgetfulness. I comforted her, and she was elected homecoming queen, with her proud father standing by her side. There were many times after that my father was not a part of special occasions, but God was always there for us. He never abandoned us.

As for me, I grew up internalizing my feelings for the most part, which is a trait that I have spent years trying to change. There are times when being reserved is beneficial, but there are other times when we need to get our feelings out in the open and not be too shy to speak and voice our opinions and feelings. When we don't express them, these feelings can become like carbonation in a soda bottle that has been severely shaken and is just waiting to be opened up so it can erupt. Are you holding in feelings that need to come out?

Do you feel like a shaken bottle of soda? If you don't feel comfortable talking with someone about the issues at hand, at least take a moment to write them down on paper. Sometimes this can be great therapy, and allows you to release those private feelings that you so desperately need to get out in the open. Then, once written, hold that paper close to your heart, and pray. Pray for God to help you with those feelings, deal with the hurts, and give you the strength and courage to forgive those who may have hurt you. Ask Him to bring comfort to you, through the peace and compassion that only your savior can provide.

After the formal separation was finalized, my dad moved into a tiny little house on the other side of town, which seemed like merely one of dozens of tiny little houses in rows and rows. The actual size of the house could have been plenty big, but in my mind it was the size of a dollhouse, certainly not a place for my daddy to live. It was not at all like our own cozy and loving home, and seemed so cold, empty, lonely and far away. Regardless of the circumstances that may have caused my parent's marriage to collapse, I could hardly sleep at night knowing that my daddy was having to stay in that little house all by himself, on the other side of town, without goodnight kisses and hugs, and home-cooked meals in the evenings. We still spent time with him, but it was never the same, for once divorce strikes a family, things can never be the same. Then the company he was employed with transferred him to Greensboro, North Carolina, and the visits became very infrequent, maybe because he had a new life, but probably primarily due to the eight hours of interstate that separated us. As time passed, his distance became a way of life.

Although my mother and siblings and I still lived in our lovely home, we struggled with the challenges daily. Even though we were young, it was obvious that my mother experienced serious emotional challenges, and eventually she had financial worries as well. She had every reason to feel depressed, hurt and abandoned, but she maintained her heart of joy and love, and I grew up hoping that one day I could be as wonderful as she was. She was always such a shining example of God's joy, despite the hardships that she endured. She tried to shelter us from the bitterness of divorce, and spent her days building our little rainbows of life while pushing aside her own. Throughout our childhood, the three of us were loved, adored, well cared for and supported, and that was what was most important.

My mother continued to take us to church, even though it was challenging for her to attend the same church without a husband now. Many times I would often put up a major fight about church attendance, but she persevered, and kept us involved in church choirs, youth groups, Sunday school classes and worship services. We attended a Presbyterian church, and when I became of age, I went through the standard confirmation class, learned scripture, prayed, took oaths and dedicated my life to the Lord. One of my most precious treasures is a little note on a small piece of yellowed torn paper, upon which I had written when I was very small, many years prior to my formal acceptance of Christ. On this little yellow tattered note, I asked God to come into my life, forgive me of my sins, and come into my heart forever. On the other side of the note was the address that I was mailing my note to—1 Heavenly Lane, Heaven.

Orange and Blue Make a Dull Shade of Brown

An orange is a popular summer fruit, well rounded, fragrant, and sweet. The color orange is often used to paint a sunshine or symbolize a bright Halloween pumpkin. For several years after accepting Christ into my heart, and as I matured and became more knowledgeable of God's word, on a child's level or course, I felt fulfilled with my Christian beliefs and this was a sweet, happy and warm time in my life. I stayed active in my church activities and had good Christian friends. That is not to say that I actually led a Christian life worthy of bringing glory to God, since at the time I really had no idea what that implied. However, at a minimum, I felt I was a good person, I had a great family, I knew Jesus was my Lord and Savior, and had confidence that I was going to heaven.

As I approached and endured the teenage years of my life, that orange glow slowly changed. Although my life was still filled with blessings and I was still grounded in my faith, you certainly wouldn't get the impression that I was a happy person, based on looking at pictures of me from that teenage era of my life. My family and I laugh now as we look back at old pictures of me, with my teenage "attitude-intense" smirk that I have on my face in most of the pictures documenting that era. During those years, I was convinced that my parents were unfair, my life was not fair, and basically, nothing was fair. Life was all about me—why couldn't they see that? That ugly shade of brown started slowly seeping into my rainbow.

I now regret that I wasted so many years not truly loving the Lord, or recognizing Him in my life. I was so consumed with what was best for me, and what I wanted, which is the case for most young girls, that I was blind to the fact that I needed to refocus my energies on more eternally significant things and the importance of family. My spiritual eyes were closed, and all I could see what was right in front of me, fair or not. Although I couldn't see it at the time, mainly because I was not looking for God's hand in my life, it is apparent that His hand was ever-present, as he miraculously carried my family through the emotional and financial hardships that existed. Many of those hardships were ones of which I was unaware existed at that time, due to my mother making every effort to keep us from worrying, nonetheless God continued to provide and protect our family.

In 1985, I graduated from high school with good grades and a long laundry list of my social and academic accomplishments, and left home to go to college. I had applied at several Georgia colleges with my friends, some of which I was accepted to, and some of which I wasn't. In the end, I was *forced* to apply to the University of North Carolina at Charlotte. My dad left my choice of college up to me; however, the only one he agreed to pay for was UNC-Charlotte. Obviously, UNC Charlotte was where I "chose" to go. My parents and my grandparents had all attended and/or graduated from UNC-Charlotte, and I was to carry on the family tradition.

Little did I know at the time that the main reason I was forced to attend this top notch college and live in the breathtakingly beautiful city of Charlotte, obtain a valuable degree and have family members within driving distance, was to give me the opportunity to expand my horizons and build a better life for myself. Although I did not realize it or acknowledge it, God was involved with the college-choosing process. God knew the plans he had for me. He knew where I needed to be, and that his choice of college was where He would lead me to meeting my soul mate.

But I, of course, in my infinite wisdom in the midst of my "all-about-me" syndrome, thought it was a deliberate and vindictive attempt by my parents to get me away from my my boyfriend at the time, whom I had every intention of marrying after 18 months of courting. I was 18 years old and felt very experienced and mature in the areas of life and love. The thought never crossed my mind that I should look at the future that this college and degree could hold for me.

Needless to say, the end of my senior year in high school and the summer prior to starting college, my mother and I were not the best of friends; instead I had convinced myself that she was the enemy. I honestly don't believe my mother did anything to deserve that type of disrespect from me, although sometimes she seemed too strict in my expert opinion (based on surveys from my friends about their mothers, and I'm not so sure that was valid information). But looking back, I know that the strict rules she required us to adhere to were based on her strong faith, her desire and maternal responsibility to teach us right from wrong, and possibly due to trying to overcompensate for not having our father at home for backup, support and fatherly discipline.

My dear mother was very strict about our dating, phone conversations and outings with friends and boyfriends, so since my dad lived in another state, she had to be the bad guy all by herself. One particular day, which was actually a repeat of many days prior, I did not get off the phone with my boyfriend when she requested it. After numerous unsuccessful attempts and at least one or two hours of waiting, she proceeded to rip the phone cord out of the wall. That incident was apparently the straw that broke the camel's back regarding my teenage phone obsession, and although I was immensely angered about it, I did end my phone conversations more quickly in the future!

Although we had our good moments and fun mother/daughter times, I suppose I could be categorized as a rebellious teenager. I did not drink, smoke, or do drugs, but I fought her at every turn, every decision, every provocative fashion trend, and challenged every rule. I feel very badly about how I treated her those last couple years, and my brother and sister at times (but I still deny the toilet incident). I just wasn't always the loving person that I knew I had inside of me. Looking back on those years, I can see that I had everything to be happy about and abundant blessings. I still have wonderfully close relationships with my parents and siblings, but back then, family was just not always at the top of the "most important things in my life that I need to treasure and not take for granted" list. I know I was just a typical teenager and that most teenagers are no different, so I have decided that the teenage years should be officially reclassified as the "I deserve whatever I think I want or need, but don't even think I'm going to appreciate it" years.

If you are reading this book and currently have strained relationships with your parents or other family members, whether you are a teenager, young adult or mature adult, I want you to consider this verse in Psalms 68:6: *"God sets the lonely in families, he leads forth the prisoners with singing; but the rebellious live in a sun-scorched land."*

God didn't invent the concept of family just so we would have people in our lives that we can share bloodlines with. A family is a blessing. Yes, families have problems, some worse than others, but they are still families. God divinely births each person into a specific family for a specific reason. But if we rebel against our families or against the rules of God, we will end up in a sun-scorched land, full of famine, droughts and death. If you are currently having problems with your parents or other family members, I encourage you to immediately make every effort to mend those relationships. Delve into God's word for strength, guidance and encouragement. Take the high road, not the "sigh" road. A heavy sigh of despair won't fix the problems, but acknowledging your part in the problems that exist and trying to take the road that Jesus would have taken, will help lead you to a renewal of love in your family.

For just a moment, try to envision your family through God's eyes...your perspective may change.

Unfortunately I chose not to view my family through God's eyes and continued to see through the warped eyes of a teenager. As a result, due to my bitterness about my parent's divorce and the standard teenage rebellion stage that I was going through in my quest to be mature and independent, somewhere along the line I entered the doors of the wilderness. I quit walking *with* God and started walking *in front* of Him. I knew He was still there, my foundational beliefs and everything I had learned in childhood were still in my heart, but I decided that I could lead the way myself. I was no longer allowing God to work in my life. Unfortunately, I fell into a gap of bad decision-making and sinful choices as a result.

We have all heard that hindsight is 20/20 and this is definitely a truthful statement. I now fully understand that when we are trying to live life our way, without God's hand in our life, we cannot *ever* win. When God's loving hands are not tightly wrapped around our hearts and souls, the devil no longer takes a back seat in our life. I'm sure that in the midst of living my life away from God, that Satan was having a big ol' party. Satan rejoiced in the fact that he had managed to steal my joy and fill me with doubts and insecurities. And once Satan has entered the doorways of our mind, he will not go out without a fight. Without a growing passion for God's word and allowing Him to be active in our life, we turn into walking targets for the devil. We might as well put a big sign on our back that plainly reads: "Take me, Satan!"

In these times when we are lost, it is so easy for the devil to attack us because we have no spiritual ammunition. It would be like a soldier walking into enemy lines without any weapons to protect himself. God's word, His power and His love for us, are our only weapons against the devil. If we don't hold onto those weapons as our most valuable resources, the devil will pull us into the enemy territory before we even know what hit us. And like any war zone, once you enter it, it is extremely unlikely that you will return unharmed.

THREE
Storing Away Necessities on the Ark

Genesis 6:19-21: *"You are to bring into the ark two of all living creatures, male and female, to keep them alive with you."*

Varying Shades of Green

My shades of blue and green were starting to change. Bright green were the times when I was just a little girl, blossoming into a young lady and learning about life. Darker green is still a state of learning, but with a little bit of experience under my belt. Then the blues crept in and caused my rainbow to begin to fade. This phase of life is one in which we start building on the foundation of our rainbow and storing up experiences that will transition us into young adulthood. Over the next few years, I would begin gradually filling my "ark" up with colors of the "arc."

In August 1985, I set off for the University of North Carolina at Charlotte with my mother and an SUV packed full of dorm room essentials. We drove over six hours from Georgia to Charlotte and met my dad at the college. The time had finally come for me to be free and to start my newest journey in life. I was scared but excited; nervous but anxious; I wanted my parents to leave, but also wanted to latch on to them like a leech and cry like a two-year-old that was getting dropped off at daycare. Through mixed emotions, we finally got everything unloaded and my dorm room arranged. The time came for me to bid farewell to my parents, at least for a few months until I would be able to go home. But for someone who was rather sheltered her entire life, who never went anywhere without leaving a specific detailed agenda of my whereabouts, and who had never spent any real length of time away from family, much less unsupervised, a few months of freedom might as well have been a few years in my mind.

My dad ended up being the last one to leave on that infamous day, mainly because my poor mother, bless her heart, was having an emotional breakdown behind the wheel of her car. For anyone who didn't see her driving off in tears, I'm sure they heard her. I remember not looking back at her as she drove away through the dorm parking lot. I didn't want her to see me crying too. I didn't want her to know that I really was scared and despite all the problems we had experienced, I didn't want her to leave and I loved her dearly. To compound these emotions, my dad was still there and I certainly didn't want to show any signs of weakness. That would be immature, right? (And I was just so mature, you know.) I'm sure that the six-hour drive back to Georgia that day was one that my mother has not forgotten. That is way too much time to spend in the car alone with your thoughts after the emotional roller coaster of leaving your first-born at college.

As I mentioned earlier, I was dating a young man during my senior year of high school and which my 18-year-old mind had determined to marry. He was a wonderful young man and cared for me deeply and we were in love. But like most young romances, it took only a few months of being in college to find out that there were a lot of fish in the sea and maybe he wasn't "the one" as I had thought. Like most young high school romances, once the college scene is in the picture, new temptations often win out over teenage love promises. In this case, distance did not make the heart grow fonder with my beau.

Eventually my visions of marrying this young man became a past memory and he was the least of my concerns. How could I be concerned about this old relationship when I was focused on my new friends, college classes, local dance clubs, dorm parties and intramural sports…and a new love interest. I'm not proud of the way it happened, but eventually I decided to break up with that boyfriend. The only problem was that somewhere along the line I sort of forgot to *tell* my boyfriend that I had broken up with him.

I was not allowed to have a telephone in my dorm room due to the traumas I had put my mother through regarding telephone usage abuse at home. I guess since she wouldn't be around to jerk the phone cord out of the wall when I had been chatting for three hours (on her long distance telephone tab), she felt that was enough justification from a parent's standpoint not to give me my own phone. So when my boyfriend called my hallmate's room asking for me, my so-called friend took it upon herself to inform him that I was seeing someone else. I still don't know what well-intentioned plan my hallmate had for ending our relationship, but this long-distance relationship thing wasn't really working to my benefit anyway and remember, life was definitely all about me. So life continued, I got over the broken relationship, but I have always felt sadness for how I must have made that wonderful young man feel. I hope that he had the strength to forgive me and in turn I eventually had to forgive my "Oh, I have to tell the truth even though nobody asked me anything" hallmate and the "someone else" that I had been seeing became a serious love interest.

I met my would-be husband, Michael, during my first month of college. He loves to tease me about the first time we supposedly met. He is one year older than me and therefore had already completed his freshman year at UNC-Charlotte, thus making him a seasoned college student when I arrived for my first day of school with sobbing parents in tow.

Students who had at least one year of college under their belt could volunteer to help new students move into their rooms on the first week of school, which allowed them to move in a day early and miss the mad rush of the official move-in date into the dorms. He was given the very important position of operating the elevator and punching the buttons of whatever floor that the new students needed to get to. He proudly claims, which I deny, that I was "giving him the eye" in the elevator that day, before we even exchanged any words, and in front of my dad, who was already wanting to put a chastity belt around me after looking at all the beer cans in the suite lobbies from parties the night before.

But not long after the romantic moment that Michael insists that we shared in the elevator, which I was unaware of, he and I hit it off. Michael was a wonderful, handsome, intelligent young man and so full of life. Everyone loved him, which is what drew me into his presence. He was always the life of the party. He was athletic and we both enjoyed spending time playing college intramural sports. One stark difference between Michael and I was that he had been a star athlete in high school and sports were never my God-given talent. So I was happy as a lark wearing the intramural football flags around my waist as long as my team didn't actually expect me to catch the ball, fall down or do any sweating! Another trait I admired about Michael was that he had a photographic memory, which was amazing, but also which annoyed me immensely. I could study for hours for a calculus test and he would read over the chapter one time. Guess who got the better grade? If you guessed that it wasn't me, you are correct! Math is definitely not one of my spiritual gifts! But God has a sense of humor and many times we are witness to the fact that opposites attract!

Since we lived in a co-ed dorm and in the same dorm suite, he and I spent a lot of time together and had the same mutual friends. Our group of friends all went out together practically every single night to various nightclubs and bars and college parties or events. It was as if we had created our own sorority/fraternity group, without going through "rush" or forking out a lot of money! But as a result, in actuality, Michael and I never really went on *a date*, we just *started dating*. After a few short months, we became a hot item and began being recognized as boyfriend and girlfriend. "Michael and Tracie" became a phrase. We were no longer just two individual people.

What Color Is Created When Colors Are All Mixed Together?

As is the case for many young kids who are experiencing their first true independent freedom, finding a church and getting involved with other students who make religion a serious part of their life in college seemed to take a back seat. I needed to make friends, fit in with the crowd, learn my way around the campus, party, attend classes and study (especially on Sundays, since most weekends I had been too pre-occupied with my own agenda to study for Monday classes or tests). All these things took so much time that going to church was not always in the schedule. Suddenly, my colors of green, blue and orange were all merging together.

Each experience so far was very important to my life and so many experiences were yet to occur. However, I was very fortunate that Michael was also brought up in church, which was another thing that strongly attracted me to him. Even though I was wandering around in the wilderness, I still knew in my heart that I wanted a Christian man. I remember calling home to my mother during my second month of college and being so excited to tell her about Michael. He not only didn't wear flip-flops and tank tops on our dates like some of my prior boyfriends, but he was a Christian! An additional benefit was that he wore loafers and golf shirts every day—not just on Sunday! But most importantly, he was raised in a Christian family and since he had grown up in Charlotte, we occasionally attended church with his family. Little did I know at that time that although Michael's parents may not have thought I was the right catch for their precious son, they would eventually become one of God's major blessings in my life and part of God's plan to bring me back into His light.

As we all know, being religious doesn't stop at going to church, it's a matter of the heart. Neglecting God is something we all do at some stage in our life and usually we don't do it on purpose. During those few years in late high school and early college, I didn't purposely fall away from God, it just kind of...happened. No matter how often I went to church, I was mainly there in body and not in spirit.

I had plenty of things to fill my time that were equally important...such as sleeping late, dating, going to whatever bar was having the best cover charge or drink specials, dancing the night away, playing flag football, laying out in the sun, oh, and occasionally attending classes and maybe even studying.

Being away at college with my newfound independence and not having to answer to anyone was too strange for words. I'm sure that every new college student experiences this same phenomenon, but some handle it better than others. I vividly remember being filled with excited adrenaline the first time I went to Bojangles and didn't have to ask anyone if I could go or tell anyone that I was going! Now I did have to count nickels in order to afford my delicious chicken biscuit, but obviously it didn't take much to excite me!

This freedom was wonderful; life was good...until first semester report cards were mailed home. As you can probably imagine, my parents were not thrilled about my grades during that first semester, or the fact that my overall GPA was barely in the two-digit category. I couldn't believe it, but my parents actually demanded some hard evidence that I had attended a class and opened a book! My dad had accurate records of hundreds of dollars he had spent on books, so he insisted on looking at them to see if the pages were even wrinkled!

I had always been a good student in high school, but I just never had this many distractions before. I had never had so much independence before either and I was taking 100% full advantage of that independence, which left 0% to focus on school.

But once my pathetic grades became public knowledge, that carefree excitement came to a screeching halt. My dad gave me the well known "Improve your grades or you are coming home" threat, which actually worked. The horror! I couldn't go home and lose my independence! Plus I knew what a college degree could mean for my future. So the next semester I made my studies more of a focus and improved my grades tremendously. Isn't it amazing what you can accomplish when you put your mind to something!

Despite my renewed interest in succeeding in college, the fact remained that the words "alcohol" and "college" go hand in hand…right? No colleges advertise this motto, but a lot of students assume this is the motto for any college and make every effort to support that motto. We wouldn't want to let our fellow students down, now would we? What would they think of me if I declined their generous offers of various beverages? What a prude I would be if I told them I was staying home to study instead of hitting the bars that night? So I did my share of participating in that favorite past time of partying and drinking, in an effort of supporting the expectations of friends and mirroring the actions of everyone around me. During high school, I didn't drink at all, so my tolerance level for alcohol was…well, non-existent. In fact, embarrassingly enough, I was pretty pitiful looking on numerous occasions, even after just a couple drinks. Sometimes my husband and I both joke that we are amazed that we lived through those four years. However, looking back at it now, it is not a joke, it is a sheer grace-of-God miracle. Even though we were not aware of it, God obviously had His angels watching over us and I shudder to think how many times those angels must have been hard at work protecting our lives and preventing harm from coming to us.

There are lots of things I would do differently if I had my life to live over, but the one thing I wish I could change most about my past is that I would treasure the one private and special gift that God gave each of us—the one thing that can never be returned after we choose to release it. What is that gift you ask? That *gift* is the sacred, precious treasure of virginity. Male or female, virginity is the one gift that can only be given away one time. Once you give that unique and personal treasure away…it is gone, forever.

An Emergence of Red

Red represents sin. Red represents the blood that was shed for us by Jesus Christ for our sins, but it also has sin written all over it. If it weren't for the red blood that Jesus Christ shed for us, we would all be doomed to an eternal life apart from God. Christians are so thankful for the red blood that was shed for us, but we still have to live with and understand that red also carries the connotation of sin.

Another word for red is scarlet, which was often used in biblical times. In the book of Matthew during the recollection of events of the crucifixion of Jesus, we are told this, Matthews 27:28, *"…they stripped him and put a scarlet robe on him".* They clothed Jesus in the color of sin. The Roman centurions and guards did everything possible to insure that they completely humiliated Jesus and since he was a pure, righteous and holy being, clothing him in the color that symbolized sin and impurity was just another way to torture Him.

Black represents evil. Evil is dark and sinister. Once we dabble in the color black, our lives will be changed forever. Red and black merged together—sin and evil—do not paint a pretty picture.

FOUR
The Flood That Destroyed Everything

Genesis 6:17: *"I am going to bring flood waters on the earth to destroy all life under the heavens, every creature that has breath of life in it. Everything on earth will perish."*

Living in the Shadows of Red and Black

All mankind are sinners. Even professed Christians who were taught proper morals and ethics, as I was, can easily get trapped into sin the minute they stop recognizing and acknowledging their sin, thus entering the wilderness far away from God. I did not become a sinner because I sinned or lost sight of the true risen Lord, but instead I sinned because I am a born sinner, which results in the act of sin as a by-product of having free will. This act of free will resulted in my life being flooded with sin and problems, never to be the same again.

Why is it that teenagers and young adults don't think that birth control really applies to them? Why is it they think that pregnancy can never happen to them? That whole story about microscopic sperm traveling to the ovaries and fertilizing a tiny egg is just so farfetched. Just because we are taught about the birds and the bees from our parents at a young age and just because the science and biology books outline every ounce of detail on how pregnancy happens; just because we were grossed out in middle school when we had to discuss the male and female anatomies and the purpose of various organs, does not mean all that stuff is actually true.

I can't think of anything my parents should have done differently to prevent me from making mistakes. They taught me values and made it clear that sex before marriage was wrong. We went to church and I was saved. I believe that over time, as a result of my immature actions, poor choices and lack of attention to my relationship with Jesus, that I simply fell far from God's will. I became lost in the wilderness of my independence, trapped in the bondage of my sin and basically at the point of not even thinking about God for months at a time. I was so far from God, that *something* had to happen to get my attention.

Please listen carefully to this following statement: God does not make bad things happen to us. No matter what we have done in life, He is not a vengeful God. In 1 Chronicles 16:34, it says, *"Give thanks to the Lord for He is good; His love endures forever."* His love is unfailing and unconditional. We may be forced to suffer the consequences of our own choices, but God is a loving God.

When we suffer painful trials that we have no control over, such as the loss of a loved one, a divorce, or a miscarriage, the right thing to do is to convince ourselves that in some bizarre way, that trial will eventually bring glory to God. We have to know it was part of His plan. But aren't we all are so quick to blame God for our misfortunes? We say to ourselves, "God, how could you let this happen to me? I have loved you and I accepted you as my savior? Why didn't you protect me from this hardship?" In times where you find yourself saying these things, please remember that God loves you and YOU are His child. His only desire is to love you and protect you and it is your joy and abundant life that He ultimately desires for you. His heart aches when He knows you are hurting. Also, if you attempt to distance yourself from God due to sadness or anger during difficult times, you will have a much harder time getting through it. God is our comfort, in happy and sad times, if we invite Him in to share in our experiences.

Genesis 2:26: *"And the Lord God commanded the man, You are free to eat from any tree in the garden; but you must not eat from the tree of knowledge of good and evil, for when you eat of it you will surely die. "* The key word here is "free." God clearly told Adam and Eve not to eat from the tree, but He gave them free will to choose whether or not to do so.

We could quickly condemn Adam and Eve for making such a stupid mistake. God himself told them they would die if they ate it, but they apparently forgot that part of His sermon! However, condemning them for acting on this poor judgment would be very hypocritical, since there is not a person alive who hasn't made terrible mistakes or bad decisions. There is not a person alive who hasn't made crude errors in judgement that they regret from the bottom of their souls.

Don't we all make mistakes and bad choices, even when we clearly know the consequences, just like Adam and Eve? After consuming the apple, Adam and Eve were ashamed, just as we are when we have to face the consequences of our sin. Genesis 2: 11 says, *"And he (Adam) answered, 'I heard you were in the garden and I was afraid because I was naked, so I hid. '"* Adam was so ashamed that He tried to hide not only his physical body, but also his sin. But sin cannot be hidden from God.

God allows us to suffer the consequences of our free will so that we can learn from our mistakes. There is no doubt that Adam and Eve learned their lesson that day, but by then it was too late to turn back. God has a plan for everything and despite our mistakes, His plan always includes the option for us to take our sufferings and turn them into a tool to bring glory to his kingdom.

For years I had a really hard time with that concept. God's punishment is one misconception that it took me years to comprehend. Consider these verses:

Hebrews 12:5 says, *"...My son, do not make light of the Lord's discipline and do not lose heart when he rebukes you,*

*because the Lord disciplines those he loves and he punishes
everyone he accepts as a son."*

James 1:2 says: *"Consider it pure joy, my brothers (and
sisters), whenever you face trials of many kinds, because you
know that the testing of your faith develops perseverance.
Perseverance must finish its work so that you may be mature
and complete, not lacking for anything."*

' If you interpret those verses, they are saying that if we are
suffering, or dealing with the consequences of our sin, we should be
thankful and happy, because God is acknowledging us as His child
and is showering his loving discipline on us. What? Thankful?
Happy? Consider my trials as a pure joy? How can I be thankful or
joyful for the terrible things that are happening in my life? The only
way we can do that is through the amazing power and grace of God.
We could never have that mindset without His supernatural power
and intervention. It is humanly impossible.

The thought of being joyful for trials is hard to swallow when you
are not active in the family of God and have strayed from your
spiritual path. God gave us the blessing of free will, so our mistakes
are our own mistakes and that blessing of free will often leads to bad
mistakes being made. But God is there to help us through those
situations and to use those situations to His glory…if we allow it.

Sometimes it can take many, many years to realize how bad
experiences and the results of sin can be used for His glory. Hebrews
12:5 and James 1:2 are so critically important for us to understand
and believe. It is the only glimmer of hope in the midst of any crisis
or need. But for those who don't know the Lord Jesus Christ as their
heavenly Father, or for those who have strayed and are abiding in the
wilderness, there is no hope and therefore a lack of understanding,
much less thankfulness, for hardships.

A Mixture of Red and Black

Okay, we have established that red equals sin and black equals Satan. When you mix those two colors together, the final outcome is not going to be pretty.

So let's go back to that whole pregnancy myth. It turns out that on one specific night in my late teenage college life, the myth of the sperm fertilizing the egg that I had subconsciously completely dismissed as a bogus claim became a reality. I didn't realize this reality until several weeks later, when I skipped a menstrual period. I convinced myself that even though I had skipped a period, there was no way that I could be pregnant. That does not happen to people like me. But I finally broke down and bought a pregnancy test.

I will never forget the very second that I saw the results on the test stick. I just stared into the bathroom mirror…for how long I don't know…it was as if time stood still. To this day, I can still see myself standing there in a trance, locked in the bathroom, looking at myself with disgust, disbelief and an overwhelming, numbing fear. There I was, 19 years old, unmarried, just finished my freshman year of college and pregnant. The horror, the shame, the guilt, the fear, the uncertainty…the baby. What would I do with a baby? I had no job, no money, no husband, no house, nothing. I still was not allowed to stay out past 11:00 p.m.!

After a couple weeks of emotional and mental torture which I could share with no one except my boyfriend, the choice was made to get an abortion. Any thoughts of keeping the baby (of course I didn't refer to the pregnancy as *a baby)* never really occurred. But I knew in my heart and soul that I should not even consider such an act—that it was wrong. But being the young girl that I was, still so dependent on my parents and their support, still in college and only on the brink of young adulthood, the immaturity, stupidity and fear in my mind won out over the crushing pain and burning morals in my heart.

Shortly afterwards, I made an appointment with an abortion clinic in a nearby city. I didn't tell my parents. I knew they would be so upset, so heartbroken, so disappointed and so ashamed. My mother had been through so much already with the divorce, financial issues, various other problems and emotional traumas (many of which I had caused) that I just couldn't bear to tell her about what I had done. Telling her would not only be admitting that I had sex outside of marriage, but that I had not been intelligent and mature enough to take precautions against pregnancy. Telling her might create doubts about the decision I had made to have an abortion and if I gave in and looked at this pregnancy as a life that deserved to be born, that would change my whole future.

I mentioned earlier that I don't have the best memory of all the things that have taken place in my life, but true life-altering events seem to be stuck in my head forever. I would do anything if I could erase these painful memories from my mind, but I know that is not possible unless I want to undergo some crazy hypnotism therapy, which is not an option! But after all these years, I can now finally explain why I have forgotten many important good childhood experiences but vividly remember this painful experience like it was yesterday. I now know that God has allowed me to store these memories in my mind forever so that my heart could be transformed and so that I would eventually use them to His Glory. But at the time this crisis was occurring, glorifying God was the farthest thing from my mind. In fact, I was very mad at God and confident that this was all His fault. I had believed in Him and this should not have happened to me. I knew I hadn't been the poster child for the best Christian the last few years, but how could He let this happen to me? Did I really deserve this cruel and harsh punishment?

Raindrops of Sorrow from Heaven/
Raindrops of Laughter from Hell

I was working as a bank teller over the summer of 1986 when I got pregnant. Another excellent decision I made was that I convinced myself that simply not showing up for work just one day would be less problematic and would be easier than calling them and trying to fake an illness or make up an excuse. I was never a good liar. But this turned out to be just one more bad decision that I learned to regret.

The pre-determined morning was cool and rainy, even though it was late June. Thinking back on this day, I believe that the weather symbolized that the heavens were weeping and our Lord was hanging his head in sorrow, knowing what I was planning to do that day to one of His children. As I made the long trip to the clinic, I was a nervous wreck, but almost in a daze. My stomach was already sick with anguish. I was in a state of not thinking, not feeling and certainly not knowing what was in store for me—not only for that day, but also for the rest of my life.

I finally arrived at the clinic and recall sitting in the waiting room. It was a gloomy, dull waiting room, filled with dozens of other women of all ages and even some little kids running around. I remember thinking that I wanted to crawl into a hole and die because anything would be better than being there in that horrible place, although it was actually a clean, normal medical facility with a standard waiting room for patients. I just wanted to get it over with quickly and put this whole nightmare behind me, but unfortunately, as God planned it, it took a painfully long time before my turn came.

As I waited, a woman sitting beside me began talking to me. I tried to ignore her. I was not in the mood to make small talk. But she continued to try to strike up a conversation with me, as if we were sitting at the Dairy Queen waiting for our Blizzards. She asked me if this was my first pregnancy. My face instantly flushed. I wanted to scream. She knew my shameful secret, but then I remembered…I was sitting in an abortion clinic; it's obvious to everyone why I am there. So I nodded yes, turned my head away from her and choked back the tears. She said with a smirk and a sigh that she already had several children, but this was her third abortion because she kept getting pregnant but she just didn't want any more children. I was absolutely sickened, shocked and appalled by her comment. How could she sit there, with a smirk on her face and say that she was killing her babies on purpose, just because she didn't feel like having any more kids? How could she be using abortion as a birth control method? How could she dispose of the life of her children as if they were an old piece of trash? What a horrible, horrible, evil and sick person! I wanted to get as far away from that demon lady as I could. But then there was I, sitting right beside her; however, I did scoot over a little to put some distance between us. How hypocritical of me to be judging her, but I convinced myself that my situation was different. I didn't want to be there, I didn't want to be doing this and I was consumed with grief, despair and guilt. I knew it was wrong and I didn't brush it off like it was my third simple root canal; I just wanted it to all go away. But regardless, we were both there for the same reason.

Finally, after what seemed like eternity, my name was called. With weak legs and the fear obviously showing on my face, I immediately started crying so hard that I could hardly speak. The nurse escorted me into a crowded room and began an IV, at which time I was still sobbing hysterically. The nurse took pity on me and began asking me if I was sure if I wanted to do this and in between sobs, I unfortunately said yes.

God tried to give me so many opportunities to leave and choose life over choice. He made me wait a very long time before my name was called and certainly gave me plenty of time to rethink this decision; He placed a lady in my path to turn my stomach with her story and make me truly consider and acknowledge the value of life and the lives of the several babies that this woman had already destroyed; He gave me a nurse who could tell I did not want to be having this procedure and who gave me an opportunity to say no and leave. He opened the door many times for me to jump up and run from that clinic of evil as fast as I could, but I kept shutting the door and allowing my fear of what this pregnancy could mean for my life to take precedence over what I knew was the right thing to do in my heart.

By this time I felt that I had come too far to turn back and I didn't know what turning back would mean. The last thing I remember before falling asleep under the anesthesia was the nurse asking me, once again, if I was sure about my decision. My emotional distress was obviously not a secret. Once again, my loving God had provided yet another door for me to exit through to escape the devil's sinister plan and one last and final chance to do the right thing. Although my lips said "yes," my heart, soul and mind screamed "no." God's heart must have broken into pieces when He heard my last and final answer. If only I had known that saying no, turning back and facing the consequences of my actions, would be the best thing for my life in the long run and certainly for the life of my unborn child. The immediate consequence of confessing to my parents what had happened and being an unmarried teenage mother would have been extremely difficult, but oh, how I wish I had made that choice.

Apparently I had continued to cry to some extent while under anesthesia, or my sobs had been temporarily just put on hold, for when I awoke after the procedure, I was still crying, almost without having control over it. It was as if I had been holding my breath and when I awoke, I gasped for breath and sobbed uncontrollably. I stayed in recovery for a while, allowing myself to have even more time to hate myself and think about what I had just done, but finally

I was able to leave the devil's haven and headed for the safe haven of home.

I returned home that afternoon looking the same on the outside, but changed forever on the inside. A part of me was missing and could never be returned. I knew there was a new littlest angel in heaven on that day. But things were never the same again.

Black Shadows Continue to Hover

Unfortunately, if you can believe it, things continued to get worse that day. Apparently not letting my employer know that I was not coming to work was just one more example of the many bad decisions I made on this day from hell. While I was missing, my employer contacted my mother asking where I was, so needless to say, she was a basket case by the time I returned home and then furious when I showed up in one piece. She was upset that I had worried her and thus she demanded an explanation.

I don't remember exactly what happened after that. I didn't confess and tell her what I had done. I put on a fake smile and just said I was sorry. I don't even remember the lame excuse I must have made up. I think I must have blocked out the memory of how much it hurt her because I don't even remember one word of our conversation. She was devastated and I could see the fear in her eyes.

Considering how well I remember every last horrible and painful detail of this experience, many of which I couldn't even mention in this book, I don't know why I can't remember talking to her. But I do recall that she called my dad and let him know about whatever it was that she knew. He had a talk with me over the phone, which I do recall. I stood in the front room of our house looking out the window at the dead grass in the yard due to the excruciating heat from the summer and listened intently.

This was probably the first serious conversation I had had with my dad in a very long time. Even though the abortion was never mentioned and I never admitted to anything, I could hear the concern in his voice as he spoke. He didn't yell at me. I would have felt better if he did. But after this day, aside from being permanently grounded, the subject was never brought up again by anyone. I wish I could say that I never thought about it again, but that is so far from the truth.

During the weeks leading up to the visit to the abortion clinic, I had convinced myself that once I took care of "the problem" that the nightmare would be over. But the nightmare did not end for me on that day, as I had thought it would; instead it was only the beginning of an even harder and more painful journey. I had thought that the fear of pregnancy was bad enough, now I knew the fear of God's wrath and the crushing fear of shame, disgust and remorse. I was more fearful of Satan than ever, knowing that the devil himself was pleased with me and nothing could be worse than that.

For months, even years, I had nightmares about babies that would race through my mind when I closed my eyes. Nightmares about babies who were hurting or crying and I couldn't help them; about the clinic; about the procedure; about the woman who had terminated multiple pregnancies for her own convenience and selfishness; about what my baby would have looked like…was it a boy or a girl? What color eyes and hair would they have had? As year after year passed, I calculated exactly how old he/she would have been that year. I knew that their birthday should have probably been around January, so each January I was reminded of my lost child and mourned for the life I had ended. Every Mother's Day as I celebrated with my dear mother, I secretly yearned for another chance to be a mother myself and my heart ached for my little child who never got to see a mother's face.

Ultimately, I was always relentlessly haunted by the searing horror of what I had done. For months I heard babies crying from time to time in my head. Every time I saw a sweet little baby out in public, I was reminded of my mistake and then again would instantly become heartbroken and devastated inside. I didn't want to visit any families that had babies in the house. Babysitting was out of the question. Every diaper commercial or just commercials with babies in them would flood my brain with the memory of what I had done to my unborn child. I truly believe that any woman with a heart who has had an abortion, or even lost a child due to miscarriage, has these same feelings of pain. These are true feelings that are hard to push aside.

Even to this day, I like to close my eyes and imagine what my child would look like, what their personality would be, what unique talents and qualities God would have given them. I often fantasize about the child I chose not to give life to—a choice that was not mine to make, as that was God's child. He/she would have been 19 years old now. Even though I didn't have the abortion out of pure selfishness or hatred or disregard for life, but rather out of immaturity and fear and ignorance, I could never forgive myself and I would never forget.

As a result of my own shame and disgust for myself, I convinced myself that God would never forgive me, much less forget, so why even bother asking? I had to allow myself to accept the punishment for my actions and therefore reluctantly conceded to live in the shadows of Satan's bondage. I honestly believed that I didn't deserve any happiness, peace or love from the Lord. So instead I held out my hands and waited for Satan to wrap his bondage around my wrists.

FIVE
The Flood Waters Begin to Rise

Genesis 7:18: *"The waters rose and increased greatly on earth and the ark floated on the surface of the water."*

Faint Shades of Orange

I have established for you that the color orange signifies warmth, the bearing of fruit and a sweet fragrance. As the months and years flew by, although my orange glow was still shadowed by red and black, the worst seemed to be over and I began to rise above the problems and painful memories and look to the future. At least now I seemed to be on top of the flood waters, instead of completely engulfed by them and gasping for air.

Five years passed and despite some typical dating problems and challenges, Michael and I continued to date throughout college. My internal sorrow for what had happened, the resentment and pain that I carried in my heart for my mistake and my bitterness towards him for his part in it, often put difficult challenges in our relationship. But our relationship eventually flourished and after awhile, I managed to toss the issue into the skeleton closet of my heart and throw away the key. I decided to leave that skeleton in there forever, never to be seen again—or so I thought. Apparently, God had a different idea in mind.

Michael and I loved each other deeply and had been through a lot together, good and bad. One summer night he surprised me by asking me to go to a special dinner and took me to a very nice restaurant. On that special evening, amid delectable food and candlelight, he asked me to marry him and I immediately said yes! He gave me a beautiful engagement ring that I treasure to this day. Everyone in the restaurant cheered; it is such a lovely memory for both of us.

I had loved Michael since the first time I saw him (which just for the record, was not in the elevator!). I ended up getting married to my wonderful husband Michael in May 1990, shortly after my college graduation (yes, I did manage to graduate with a GPA to be proud of). We were married in a beautiful church wedding in the small country church that my parents were married in. Then my new in-laws sent us to Hawaii for our honeymoon, which is a memory that we can hold dear in our hearts for a lifetime.

But even though we had a lovely wedding, incredible honeymoon and optimistic marriage anticipations, the first year of marriage was not the 12-month fairytale love story that I had in mind. Once reality set in, we moved into our new house, we had to work, we had to pay bills, etc., and things just didn't seem quite as romantic as I had hoped. Many couples have this same rude awakening after a honeymoon and we were no exception. Young people need to watch more episodes of Luci and Desi, where life, marriage and mistakes go hand-in-hand, instead of watching soap operas and love-stricken movie stars, which portray marriage as a romantic fantasy world. But despite some challenges, we loved each other and continued to build our life together as husband and wife.

We had built a house of our own which was a wonderful blessing for us, but also caused some strife between us. Surely the type of door handles we selected and the color of carpet was most certainly going to make a difference in our lives forever! But as we grew accustomed to marriage and the sacrifices required, our love grew. After three years of marriage, we decided to try to get pregnant and despite my unspoken fears of infertility, I was pregnant within three months.

For the next nine months, I carried a secret fear in my heart that something was surely going to happen to my baby in utero. In my first trimester, I had experienced some light bleeding and the only advice that my gynecologist could provide was to stay off my feet and pray for the best. I lay there during that following afternoon and night, waiting for the worst to happen, knowing that the time had come for God to inflict horrible pain and punishment on me. I knew I deserved his merciless punishment and retribution for my sin, so I just cried and prayed for Him to have mercy on me and my unborn child.

For the next six months, I feel sure that my gynecologist probably wanted to send me for a battery of psychological testing due to the countless weekly times that I called him with every ache and pain. But I was convinced that with each ache and pain would come the dreaded loss of my baby. But thankfully, I did get through that temporary bleeding problem and in January 1994, I gave birth to our first child, a seven-pound, one-ounce, curly black-headed, beautiful perfect baby girl, whom we named Morgan Ashley.

A Golden Arc Is Born

For any woman who has given birth to a child, the miracle of childbirth is phenomenal, amazing and overwhelmingly emotional. But having Morgan meant far more to me than just having a baby. I was literally consumed with instant love for her and amazed at the perfection of such a tiny human. Each time I looked at her, my heart would beat like a huge bass drum with joy and thankfulness. But something else was consuming my heart as well. Giving birth to this perfect little tiny baby, with all ten fingers and toes and perfect in every way, eliminated the consuming, unbearable, crushing fear that I had carried in my heart for nearly eight years—the fear that I would never be able to have a baby as a result of having the abortion.

For eight years I had been stricken with the daily fear that either God would punish me for committing such a terrible sin or the surgery would have damaged my uterus, preventing me from being able to get pregnant or carry to full term. But now I had given birth to a healthy baby girl and in turn a faint golden arc in my rainbow started to glow.

It has taken years to fully accept this fact, but now I can honestly say that I understand that God does not punish us out of anger, even when we so deserve it. It took the birth of this child for me to finally accept that realization and begin to understand God's unconditional mercy, love and grace.

From the day we brought Morgan home from the hospital, I worshiped and adored her. I was just so in love with her. I was also extremely over-protective of her, to the extent that it surpassed normal motherly protection. One day when she was a few weeks old, I nearly had an emotional breakdown because I accidentally made her finger bleed when I was trying to cut her tiny little newborn fingernails. I didn't want to do anything to bring her an ounce of suffering. I had already caused one child enough suffering to last an eternity.

I know that our family members thought I was obsessed with baby Morgan and probably thought I needed some professional counseling as well. The reason for that is that I would never let Morgan out of my sight for a moment. I didn't want anyone to hold her or take care of her except for me. I had a hard time even sharing her with my husband and had difficulties allowing him to even care for her basic needs. I didn't want her in a different room from me. Even if my arms fell off from fatigue, I couldn't bathe for six months, or I didn't get to sleep for a full year, this was my baby. This was my precious treasure that God had given me, even though I didn't deserve it. And if the grandparents even uttered the words, "Can Morgan spend the night at our house?" the opportunity for a panic attack was imminent.

This precious child was not leaving my sight and I was spending every possible waking moment with her. I thought maybe I could make up for what I had done eight years ago, by being the most devoted mother in the universe. No one could possibly understand how precious she was to me. No one could understand that this tiny little infant child was the primary reassurance in my life that God did not hate me. No one could understand the beautiful florescent light that shone from her face that only I could see—which was the light of God starting to seep into my heart again.

In retrospect, I recognize that I was obsessed, overly protective and actually very selfish with her. This was the first grandchild for both sides of our family and we were blessed with devoted grandparents who loved her as much as we did and just wanted to spend time with her. But my selfishness was based solely out of love, undying gratification and thankfulness for her.

I believe that my obsession with this baby was a step in the right direction to healing my heart and mending my soul. As I looked into her big blue eyes, smelled the sweetness of her curly, soft hair and ran my fingers against her perfect and soft pink skin, I knew that God couldn't possibly despise me. He couldn't really be feeling disgust at the sight of me. For if He did, He would never have allowed me to bring this precious angel into the world. He would never have given me another chance to give life to one of His children, to entrust me with her care and to be so abundantly blessed with her presence. He must have had some compassion left for me, the ugly, ultimate, broken sinner.

The cloud over my heart that had been blocking my rainbow slowly began to dissipate.

SIX
The Dove of Life Appears

Genesis 8:10: *"He waited seven more days and again
sent out the dove from the ark. When the dove
returned to him in the evening, there in its beak
was a freshly plucked olive leaf! Then Noah
knew that the water had receded from the earth."*

Michael and I grew in our role as parents, in the same "learn as you go" method that all new mommies and daddies experience. Even though we were loving parents and loved our new baby daughter, don't be fooled into thinking that after a few months of sleeplessness that there weren't many a night that we would rather spend fifteen minutes arguing about who was going to get up in the middle of the night for a feeding, or who was going to change the diaper, when we could have done both of those things and been back to sleep in the same amount of time we spent arguing about it! Everything is a game of give and take and it took a while for us to figure that out. Parenthood is definitely a ladder of learning. But this didn't deter us from our love for children and in August 1996, God blessed us again with another little angel, whom we named Kaitlyn Elizabeth.

Kaitlyn was a big baby, weighing in at over nine pounds, but again so beautiful and perfect. The only problem was that Kaitlyn decided to wait until her exact due date to be born and then decided to come without a moment's hesitation. I had hoped for natural childbirth with all my children, but not so natural that I couldn't have an epidural! Kaitlyn had decided to be punctual and in a hurry, so when I arrived at the hospital at 11:30 p.m. after fighting back fears that the baby was going to be delivered in the car and thanking God that it wasn't rush hour, a wide-eyed nurse greeted me outside.

She hurried me along and enlisted others to help speed up the process of getting me to the maternity ward. She then asked me if I needed anything. I immediately blurted out the words, "Yes! I need an epidural!"

She immediately replied with the words, "Oh, honey, it's too late for that." I instantly entertained evil thoughts of hurting that nurse on my way into the delivery area or possibly running her over with my wheelchair, but fortunately for both of us, I refrained from doing that. Kaitlyn was born within an hour of arriving at the hospital and was a healthy, gorgeous, blue-eyed blonde bundle of joy.

As always, the pleasure of being a mother causes the memories of the birthing pain to quickly fade and in September 1999, little Michael came into the picture at seven pounds and one ounce. Unfortunately, Michael was in an even bigger hurry than Kaitlyn had been and arrived a month premature, but we were so excited to have a little boy! My husband was already calling the golf pro-shop to check on the price of miniature golf clubs.

Little Michael, as we so fondly call him, was perfect, just as the girls had been, with the exception of one small problem. Since he still needed another month in the womb, his little lungs just weren't ready for the real world yet.

As soon as he was born, the medical staff began the normal procedure of cleaning out his mouth and nose and trying to get him to take his first breath and cry. But he didn't cry; instead he was breathless and lifeless. The nurses immediately took him over to another prep area in the room and I began hearing an unusual pounding noise. I soon realized that the harsh, repetitive pounding sound that was echoing in the room was the sound of the nurses beating his tiny little back trying to get him to breathe. After several minutes of this process, which I considered torture for my baby whom I could barely see through my tears, I was convinced that they were surely going to crush his tiny spine. Finally when the nurses realized their efforts were in vain, Michael was rushed out of the delivery room into NICU. I thought to myself, *Okay, the time has come for God to punish me. I already have two beautiful children, so I guess trying for three children was asking for just a little bit too much mercy from God.*

We were all in shock. I had just given birth to a beautiful baby boy and he was nowhere to be seen. I had barely had a chance to memorize what his little face looked like before he was taken from my arms and whisked away. Instead of enjoying those precious moments right after delivery when you are supposed to be cuddling your little bundle of joy, I was left empty-handed. Instead my baby was in another room, out of sight, with his new life in the hands of nurses, doctors and God. I found myself thinking, *How could this be happening? This is not how I envisioned the birth of my little son.*

In the silence, Michael and I sat there, after we had been abruptly left in the delivery room alone, weeping and scared. Our family was informed of his birth and quickly came in to see us. Without a moment's hesitation, my father-in-law began praying aloud and pleading for the life of my son, his grandson. This simple but wonderful prayer not only broke the ice of the painful silence and dissipated the cloud of fear that hung in the air, but the room was suddenly filled with prayer and with God's presence. A peace washed over me and although my eyes were still red and swollen from tears, I knew in my heart that little Michael would be fine. I don't think my father-in-law knew how much that prayer meant to me or how much I appreciated the Godly man that he was, but this prayer was another small stepping stone in the bridge that God was building for me to overcome the flood and make it safely to the other side.

After a short while, the nurses did come back into the delivery room and informed us that little Michael was fine and would certainly survive, but he needed to stay in NICU for a few days. They eventually took us down to the NICU to see him. I started sobbing all over again when I saw his frail little body lying in the incubator, unclothed, hooked up to tubes and under a bright light for warmth. I hungered to put his tiny new blue outfit on him and cuddle him in my arms, but instead I could only caress his soft pink skin. One of the nurses came by and saw me crying and she reassured me that he was going to be fine and that he merely needed a few days to adjust to his new surroundings.

Only by the grace and mercy of God, three days later I was able to put his little homecoming outfit on his tiny body and take little Michael home safe and sound and breathing perfectly. My heart went out to all the tiny babies that were still in NICU dealing with more serious problems and the parents who would have to endure even more pain and fear. But I was so thankful to be leaving there once and for all, and so thankful for the mercy God had placed over my son's life…and on my life, once again.

Now my family is complete—two girls and a boy. My goodness, how abundantly God had blessed me. But why? Why did I deserve this unmerited mercy? What had I ever done to deserve these three precious little ones? God had blessed *ME*, the person who ended the life of one His children just a few years earlier. The same God that I had so deliberately offended had given me a wonderful and devoted husband and three perfect, healthy, beautiful, blonde, blue-eyed angels, who were all the loves of my life.

Occasionally, despite my overwhelming happiness and gratitude for the joy that God had allowed me to have, I will still catch myself looking into their angelic faces and envision what my first beautiful child must have resembled. I can now put a face with the angel that I know is ever present in my life, that watches over my children and that sometimes I sense is near me when I see something out of the corner of my eye, but when I look, there is no one there.

I now know that he or she would have had big blue eyes, blonde hair, their father's nose and my dimple in their chin. I know that God has the privilege of looking into that child's sweet face every day and I can't wait to get to heaven one day and see him or her for myself. I can't wait to tell them how much I have loved them all these years.

SEVEN
The Littlest Angel

Genesis 8:15: *"Then God said to Noah, Come out of the Ark,
you and your wife and your sons and their wives.
Bring out every kind of living creature that is with you...."*

Children Add Color to Our Rainbows

I do believe in angels. The Bible tells countless stories of angels coming to earth and speaking to people to deliver God's messages.

Genesis 28:12 is a story of Jacob's dream. It reads, *"He had a dream in which he saw a stairway resting on the earth, with its top reaching to heaven and the angels of God were ascending and descending it."*

In 1 Peter 1:12, it reads, *"It was revealed to them that they were not serving themselves but you, when they spoke of the things that have now been told you by those who have preached the gospel to you by the Holy Spirit sent from heaven."* Even angels long to look into these things.

There are also countless other stories of angels appearing to people in Jesus' time. Although angels are not so commonly seen with the human eye in this day and age, don't fool yourself into thinking they don't exist.

God told Noah to gather up everything and bring it out of the ark. God told me to gather up everything out of my life that would help me to rebuild my rainbow. So I decided to recognize the angels in my life, which God wanted to bless me with.

Angels are ever present in our lives. Many times, an angel may be in the form of someone who called you to say they were thinking about you at the exact moment you needed some encouragement, or someone who takes food to a family who had just run out of money and was wondering where the next meal would come from. But angels are also present in spirit and are all around us, to protect us and nurture us, all the while remaining unseen.

I truly believe with all my heart,that my little child's soul, which didn't have an opportunity to live on planet earth, was divinely "assigned" to my family and is watching over my children from heaven as their guardian angel. This is another one of the many gifts that God has given me despite my mistakes and sins. My littlest angel started showing her presence shortly after Kaitlyn was born.

Kaitlyn was officially named the "Boo Boo Queen" when she was just a toddler. This is a title that she does not think fondly of now that she is nine years old, but regardless it is still her nickname (in addition to Katybug!).

Her first boo-boo was actually my fault and it was worse than the time that I had accidentally clipped Morgan's fingernails too closely. Kaitlyn was only a few days old and I was bathing her before we were going out somewhere. I was fully dressed and was preparing to get her dressed as well. I gently lifted her out of the sink, which was her makeshift tub since she was so small, and I went to lay her down on her towel. Unknown to me, the remnants of her still-attached little infant belly button had become snagged on the button of my shirt and was ripped off when I put her down! Oh, how she cried and cried as the blood poured out of her little wound, but my wails of sobs and tears far exceeded any crying she could do! But thank goodness her little belly button is perfect today and she doesn't remember that trauma. Now, doesn't the fingernail episode pale in comparison to this lovely memory? I don't think I will rank that experience up with the joys of motherhood.

My husband and I have decided that God gave us Kaitlyn as a special gift, to teach us to learn to handle emergencies with peace and sanity, but also to increase our faith in Him and truly believe what He is capable of doing on this earth. Let me share Kaitlyn's story briefly that earned her the "Boo Boo Queen" title.

At 18 months old, as she toddled around in an attic while my mother and I searched for something, she fell through a small hole in the second-story attic floor and landed in the garage about 15 feet below her, with no injuries; at two years old she jumped off the bed and bent the bones in her arm but did not break it; at three years old she managed to pull an entire grandfather clock down on top of her but she miraculously ended up inside the clock unharmed; at four years old she fell through a glass tabletop and had to have 18 stitches in her chin and neck and although she suffered intense bleeding, the cut just missed a major artery; at five and six she had many less serious boo-boos which are too many to list, but at least they didn't involve the annual emergency room visit; at seven years old she was squatting down on her legs, lost her balance and fell backwards at just the right angle to slash her head on a chair, then she bled profusely until the liquid stitches were secure.

I would imagine that the littlest angel of our family is thankful that most recently Kaitlyn has been free of major accidents! But it was Kaitlyn's first serious accident that I began to allow myself to believe in God's heavenly angels and that my very own littlest angel was forever in our presence.

Looking back on the very second that Kaitlyn fell from that second-story attic at 18 months of age, down a hole which we didn't know was there, I frantically rushed to where she was toddling around just two seconds earlier, leaned over and noticed the hole for the first time. With horror, I looked down as I witnessed her plunging to the hard concrete floor below. But with my own eyes, when her fall came to an end, I saw her literally bounce off of the hard concrete floor of the garage like a big rubber ball. It was as if she had landed on a big fluffy pillow of cotton and just bounced off of it. Kaitlyn had a small bruise on her forehead, but not a scratch, serious bruise, concussion or broken bone in her tiny little fragile body.

How is that humanly possible? Even the doctors could not understand it and they questioned my husband and me as to whether or not she had really fallen 15 feet. Especially since by the time we got to the hospital, Kaitlyn had stopped crying and was just acting like a normal happy baby—less than 30 minutes after falling 15 feet onto a hard concrete floor. She was happy and uninjured and pulling at the doctor's stethoscope as if she were there for a routine checkup.

There is no other explanation for this phenomenon than God's hand at work. Our little angel of mercy was with Kaitlyn that day and there is no doubt that something besides the hard concrete floor stopped her fall. Even to this day, Kaitlyn is my little prayer warrior. I know God has special plans for her life and I can't wait to see what they are. Many times when I have had to punish or scold Kaitlyn for something, I will go into her room later to find her down on her knees, praying for forgiveness and strength for God to help her change her ways. In her childlike mind, even though the sins were small or maybe even insignificant, she knows that God is her redeemer and her heart is convicted. We can learn so much from our children.

Children are a gift from God and we should never forget that for a moment. Kaitlyn's story is just one shining example of how God values His children and He wants to protect them. When we are stressed over daily challenges, when our children are healthy, sick or have long term health problems; and when our children are toddlers, teens or grown adults and yes, even when we are young, unmarried and pregnant—God wants to hold us in His arms and take care of us. Children are precious to our heavenly Father and we must never forget what a gift from heaven they truly are. We must not forget that we are His children and He loves us more than we could ever love our own offspring. I encourage you not to ever take lightly the gift of a baby growing in a uterus and to be a witness to others about this, even if it threatens your own personal popularity or if it will affect the plans that you thought you had for your life. I know all too well now that God's plans are not our plans. Proverbs 19:21 says, *"Many are the plans in a man's [or woman's] heart, but it is the Lord's purpose that prevails."* And believe me, He will prevail one way or the other!

Let me plainly tell you in three words what I believe our philosophy on abortion should be—IT IS WRONG. Period. End of story. In the book of Jeremiah, Jeremiah states that the Lord spoke to him and told him "before I formed you in the womb, I knew you." The Lord could not have known him, had he not already been a person in his mother's womb. We each have an identity that only God knows, before our physical flesh is even formed in the belly of a woman. And once the flesh is formed in the womb, no matter how tiny, God already knows the souls of the unborn. Babies are babies at the moment of conception and not a second later. The pro-choice groups, media and even our government try hard to convince the world that abortion is not a sin, that a fetus is not a baby and that we are allowed freedom of choice, regardless of the consequences. But consider just a few of the many biblical references about murder, a.k.a, abortion:

Exodus 30:12: *"Thou shalt not murder."*

Deuteronomy 5:17: *"You shall not murder."*

Matthew 5:21: *"You have heard that it was said to the people long ago, Do not murder and anyone who murders will be subject to judgement."*

James 2:11: *"For he who said, Do not commit adultery, also said, Do not murder. If you do not commit adultery but do commit murder, you have become a lawbreaker."*

Okay—so the Bible makes it clear that abortion, also known as murder to unborn children, is wrong. But unfortunately I didn't refer to these verses when I was faced with making the choice of life or death. Instead, I allowed myself to get caught up in the cultural belief that I had a right to make my own choice and fear beat out rational thinking.

But, dear one, despite the fact that abortion is morally and ethically wrong, it IS NOT the unpardonable sin. It is not a sin that puts up steel bars in front of your gateway to heaven leaving you without a key. It does not have to be a sin that keeps you away from God. Most importantly, it is not a sin that will prevent God from loving you unconditionally. You are His child, regardless of your mistakes.

John 2:1-2 says: *"My dear children, I write this to you so that you will not sin. But if anybody does sin, we have one who speaks to the Father in our defense—Jesus Christ, the Righteous One. He is the atoning sacrifice for our sins and not only for ours but also the sins of the whole world."*

Friend, take heart in knowing that no sin is too great for God to forgive. Whether your sin is abortion, adultery, theft, murder or little white lies, God wants to forgive you and make you whole again. For those who have terminated pregnancies or lost children due to pregnancy complications, miscarriage, injury or accidents, the Bible tells us that we are not only forgiven, but that we will see those little children one day in His presence. Our heavenly father has such compassion, graciousness and empathy for the parents who have lost a child, regardless of the reason or circumstance which caused them to cease living on earth, that He has given us the promise of being reunited with them and holding them in our arms.

Consider the story of King David in the book of Samuel. Simply put, one day David saw Bathsheba bathing, thought she was beautiful, decided he wanted her and then seduced her and slept with her, but to his surprise, Bathsheba conceived a child in that night of romance. Since he was in love with Bathsheba, who was married to Uriah, David made the intelligent decision to help Bathsheba become a widow, thus available for him, by having Uriah killed on the battlefield. Then he proceeded to take Bathsheba as his wife and she bore a son. When the prophet Nathan confronted David about his sin, David admitted he had sinned against the Lord and repented. His repentance is symbolic of the fact that David actually was a godly man at heart; he had just allowed himself to get caught up in worldly desires and as a result made some horrific decisions.

David had committed murder in a roundabout way, by planning Uriah's death and the Bible tells us that God was not happy with David's actions. Second Samuel 11:27 says: *"...But the thing David had done displeased the Lord."* Nathan informed David that as a result of his sin, that his new son would die and shortly after, the son became ill. David pleaded for God's mercy on his son, fasted and refrained from bathing for many days. On the seventh day after hearing the prediction of his son's death from Nathan, David's son died.

As soon as David became aware that his son had died, he quit crying and fasting. This seemed very odd to his servants and they asked him why he was no longer weeping. Why would someone weep why their loved one was alive and feast after they passed away? But David had a reason and he replied, in 2 Samuel 12:23: *"But now that he is dead, why should I fast? Can I bring him back again? I will go to him, but he will not return to me."* David's faith was so strong, that he knew that he would one day see his son again in heaven, even though it was the consequences of his own actions which had caused his son to die.

Although he did mourn his son's death, David was already looking forward to the reunion that he would one day have with his son, when he himself entered the gates of heaven. Despite David's sin and poor choices, he was confident in His savior. He knew the mercy and grace and love of the Lord. This story gives us all encouragement that one day we will see our loved ones again in heaven and we will be reunited with them. They can't return to us, but we can go to them and spend an eternity holding them in our grasp.

But even though we can have peace knowing that we have the Lord's compassion, wouldn't things be a lot easier if we just made the right choices to begin with?! I encourage you not to let the world's views infiltrate your mind and change what you know is right and wrong. Despite what your religious or personal beliefs may be, you must know deep in your heart and soul that taking a life is wrong.

I pray that you will earnestly pray for your strength and stamina in fighting against this area of sin and I hope that you will be willing to be a spokesperson for God regarding the life of unborn children, if given the opportunity. If you don't agree that abortion is wrong, I would like to suggest that you visit the internet and type in the word abortion in the images section of a search engine. The pictures that will be displayed across your screen will make you sick to your stomach and you will quickly want to close out the screen. No sane person can see those pictures and not believe that those were little babies before they were aborted. If you have found yourself in a situation in which you are pregnant and trying to make a life-changing decision of abortion versus keeping the baby, before taking any action, schedule an appointment for an ultrasound. Once you see a tiny little heart beating inside your belly, surely you will be overcome with the need to make the right decision—the decision for life.

As a preemptive measure, I pray that young girls and young women will fight the temptation of sex before marriage and thus avoid ever being put in the situation of having to consider what is right and wrong regarding this subject. I pray that adults will stand up for pro-life. You must believe that one voice and one person can make a difference. YOUR voice can make a difference. You don't have to be a celebrity to be heard and seen.

I once attended a major league baseball game at Camden Yards in Baltimore, Maryland. There was a young man at the game who was making a spectacle of himself, wearing a bathing suit and shoes. He was not wearing a shirt, but had a beach towel tied around his neck, with the words "WAVE MAN" written across the towel in black marker. It was very entertaining as he relentlessly tried to get the crowds to do "the wave," where people stand and raise their arms in perfect sequence so it appears that the crowd has a wave gently rolling through the stadium.

He began this challenge at the very beginning of the first inning and put forth unbelievable effort to meet his goal. But after a couple of hours, we went from being entertained and enthralled by him to feeling extreme pity for him as his efforts to build the wave seemed completely hopeless. We all began to hope that he would just give up and sit down in his seat and avoid any future humiliation. But he continued using every means that he could think of to get the wave started in this huge stadium, including strategically positioning friends at different parts of the stadium and then calling them on their cell phones when the wave would be getting close to their section of people, so that they could then elicit the wave from the group in front of where they were standing.

In the ninth inning, amazingly enough, his hard work paid off! We sat in awe as we watched thousands and thousands of people stand up and do the wave around the entire Camden Yards stadium and not only once, but nine times!

This is such a lesson in life for all of us. This one individual, who was unknown, unnoticed and unimportant to the whole scheme of the ballgame, was able to get thousands of people to listen to him and follow his lead! It was incredible to witness how one person was able to influence an entire major league baseball stadium to get on board with his goal! Needless to say, he was ecstatic with his accomplishment!

Let's consider this experience as an analogy of what one person could do for our world today, if only they were willing to stand up and lead! It only takes one person to make a difference. Remember the *Roe v. Wade* court case, January 22, 1973? Jane Roe was unmarried and pregnant and thought that her rights were being violated by the law which forbid her to get an abortion in her home state of Texas. So she hired a lawyer and went to court and we all know the rest of the story.

This lady was no different than you or me. She was just a regular individual, unknown to the public eye, trying to live the best life possible. The only dramatic difference between Jane and the rest of us was that she was willing to take a stand. She fought for what she thought were her rights and as a result she changed our country forever. Unfortunately the stand she took was morally and ethically wrong, but regardless, her voice made a difference in our world. As a result, she paved the way for millions of other women to have the right to make the wrong choice and millions of babies have not been given a chance to live since 1973.

What about the individual who fought for religion to be removed from public schools and now our children cannot pray or worship during their school day? The teachers are not encouraged or allowed to be strong Christian mentors for children who so badly need to know the Lord loves them. What about the person who was offended because the Ten Commandments were posted outside a courthouse and fought to have them removed? What about the person who tried to take the word God out of our country's national anthem?

As you can see, despite what the subject matter may be, it only takes one person to make a difference. Are you willing to allow God to use you to make a difference? Maybe God only wants to use you to make a difference in the life of one other person…maybe He wants to use you to change thousands of lives…maybe He wants to use you to witness to young girls and women about pro-life…maybe He wants to use you to save the life of your own unborn child, grandchild, niece or nephew…maybe He wants to use you to change our country. Will you give Him a chance to use you?

Regardless of the depth of the problem, the power of an individual and of one voice is nothing without the power of God. Although the young man who successfully got the wave going at a baseball game did not make a significant impact on our society or our world, he is an example of how one person can make a difference. If he could succeed with his goal, imagine what we could do with the power of God behind us!

Stand up for your beliefs, even if it means you will experience hardship or criticism as a result. Take a stand for unborn children and any other atrocity in today's society. Just because the world has turned an immoral act into an accepted practice does not mean that we have to support it or allow it to become the norm. The consequences of sin will be much harsher than the consequences of choosing to follow your faith. Hardships come and go, but the memories of painful sins stick with us forever.

Also, please keep in mind that even though abortion is a subject that people do not like to discuss, our children need to be told that it is wrong. Most parents want to shelter their children's innocent little minds from even knowing that abortion exists, but eventually they will hear about it and the moral groundwork needs to be firmly laid in their minds.

This issue is not just a female issue—remember about that sperm and egg myth! It takes two to tango! Boys and girls both need to know deep in their soul that abortion is wrong and is an irreparable act of sin. It's not only daughters that need to be educated about this subject, but sons as well.

My heart breaks for the young boys and girls yet to experience the task of making the decision between life and death for their unborn child and I want to do everything possible to do my part in educating our youth and society. That is one of the ways that I want to allow to God to use me. Will you join me?

EIGHT
Searching for the Rainbow

Genesis 9:20: *"Then Noah built an altar to the Lord and, taking some of all the clean animals and clean birds, he sacrificed burnt offerings on it."*

Shades of Bright Yellow

Yellow can represent a warm glow from a nightlight that keeps you feeling safe at night. It can represent the warmth of a golden summer sunshine. It can represent a pot of shiny gold coins at the end of the rainbow. At this time in my life, a faint shade of yellow started to appear.

For the first ten years of my marriage, when blessings were abounding over us in so many ways and although we were involved in our church, I still could not understand why God would have blessed me so much....not after what I had done so many years ago. In my mind, the abortion was as recent to me as what I had for breakfast that morning. The years had not erased the guilt, the shame or the painful memories. There is an old saying that "time heals all things," but without forgiveness and love and compassion from our Lord Jesus Christ, all the time in the world can't heal a broken soul.

Michael and I have been married for over 16 years now. We have persevered through all the trials that have come up against us and we are still very happily married. In fact, we are happier now than we have ever been. We have a love and respect for each other that has taken years to build. We still have our quarrels and differences of opinions, but we have both mastered the art of knowing when to push for a win and when to back off and respect each other's opinion. I also attribute this to my experiences with Proverbs 31 Ministries, in their teachings of being submissive to our husbands and being a godly wife and mother.

The word "submissive" was formerly a word that would instantly make horns sprout out of my skull. But once I allowed God to become the center of my life, I knew that I had to submit, to God and to my husband. We can't pick and choose what areas of the Bible we want to follow. The Bible is an "all or nothing" agreement. Since submission is a biblical command, I had no choice but to abide. Now keep in mind, that "submit" doesn't mean to be a doormat, it merely means to willingly yield to another. Ephesians 5:21 says: *"Submit to one another out of reverence for Christ."* And Colossians 3:18 says: *"Wives, submit to your husbands, as is fitting in the Lord."* Lastly, James 4:7 says: *"Submit yourselves, then, to God. Resist the devil and he will flee from you."* Submission is an act of love for our husbands, but also an act of love for our Lord.

When I finally gave in and gave submissiveness a try, my relationship with my husband flourished. Not because he was in control, but because my heart and attitude were changed and my love for him made me want to submit. I wanted to please him and make him proud of me and love me. After all, he was the central most important person in my life, aside from God. There are still times when those horns try to flare up, but I try to pull them back in before they do any serious damage!

I fully attribute out lasting love completely to the fact that God is now a focus in our marriage and our family. A few years ago, I finally came to realize that if God is not a priority in your marriage, then marriage is not a priority in your life. It is impossible for a marriage to survive without seeking God's will and provision for your relationship. It is impossible to have arguments with your spouse and then be willing to ask for his/her forgiveness, even when you know they were in the wrong, without a relationship with God. It is impossible to forgive our spouses for their mistakes, when we don't ask God to forgive us for our own faults first. It is impossible to forgive ourselves for our sins, be able to love ourselves and therefore love our spouses, until we ask for God's forgiveness for our own sins.

1 Corinthians 7:2-4: *"But since there is so much immorality; each man should have his own wife and each woman her own husband. The husband should fulfill his marital duty to his wife and likewise the wife to her husband. The wife's body does not belong to her alone but also to her husband. In the same way, the husband's body does not belong to him alone but also to his wife."*

God gave us a spouse for the sole purpose of becoming one. It is our marital responsibility to treasure our husbands each and every day, despite whether or not they will pick their up their dirty socks, hang up their bath towels, bathe the kids or vacuum the floor. Despite the fact that we may constantly fight over money, child rearing, or whether or not we actually "needed" the most recent outfit we purchased, we still must put our husbands at the top of our priority list. Marriage is a commitment, not just a signed piece of paper, and we must maintain a passion for Jesus in order for our passion for our husbands to endure the struggles that occur in every marriage. It is imperative that our marriages be committed to God, if we expect them to be happy, successful and fulfilling.

After years of trial and error, God made this plainly clear to me one day at the car wash. Yes, the car wash! God is not too picky about where He performs miracles!

One particularly stressful day, feelings of sadness and hopelessness had begun to engulf me. I determined that things just were not going the way I had planned in my marriage, so in my despair, I thought to myself that maybe I should pray about my problems and hand them over to God! What a revelation! I soon began praying fervently for weeks about my marriage, husband, family, relationships, job issues, children and anything else that I felt God needed to "fix" for me.

A few weeks later, on a beautiful spring day, after my husband and I had had yet another heated disagreement about some trivial issue, I was feeling extremely discouraged and frustrated. I went ahead with my plans to run some errands to get my mind off things and planned a visit to the carwash (which my husband will gladly attest to the fact that this was very out of the norm for me since I could go weeks without even noticing my car was in dire need of a bath!).

While driving to the car wash, I had once again been praying about my marriage, our strained relationship and daily struggles, and how I just did not know what to do to make things better for all of us. I was at my wit's end and feeling hopeless and broken. Little did I know that my brokenness was exactly what God had been waiting for. My desperation for His intervention opened the door for God to step into my life.

I arrived at the car wash, ended my prayer and the pity party I had thrown myself, paid the attendant and slowly walked into an empty waiting room, feeling overwhelmingly discouraged and downhearted. After a few minutes of staring aimlessly at the wall, I settled into my chair and began to take in my surroundings and glance around the room. My heart almost leapt out of my chest when I looked down at the table beside me and there was the book, *The Power of a Praying Wife*. Thank goodness I was the only person in that waiting room, because I immediately broke down into tears with shock, disbelief and an unfounded gratitude that God had sent me the answer to my prayers. Not just an answer, but a hard copy answer that I could physically grasp! I folded my hands and closed my eyes and began to pray right there in that waiting room, with no concern of whether or not anyone came in and saw me. I thanked God for answering my prayer in such a tangible way that there was no other explanation but His divine miracle. Only His powerful hand could have caused a Christian woman to visit the car wash just before I did, to accidentally leave this specific book there and then to nudge me to visit the car wash for the first time in months.

This book was the answer I was looking for and it was confirmation that God had heard my prayers. I now knew that God wanted me to continue praying and that in His time he would answer my prayers. But most importantly, through this little miracle, He showed me that I needed to pray for *MY* heart and pray that God would fix *ME*, not my husband or my circumstances. He wanted me to understand that I needed to become the godly wife that He wanted me to be, so that I could have the happy marriage that I desired. *I* needed to become more Christ-centered, if I wanted my marriage to be Christ-centered.

I still find myself from time to time desiring that God will fix the faults of my husband so that life will be better for me, but I try to remind myself that if I am looking for a solution, I need to look up to God and then inward to my own heart. I've heard my children say that when you point a finger at someone, you actually have four fingers pointing back at you! We need to look in the mirror before we take on the task of pointing out someone else's faults.

Now back to the unanswered question: Why would God give me a faithful loving husband who was a great provider, hard worker and loving father, a lovely home, wonderful family, loving in-laws and three beautiful, wonderful, healthy children? Why would He give me a good paying job that allowed me to work a flexible schedule to spend time with my children and be a devoted mother and employee? Why did He give me a beautiful home with warm beds, where there is always food in the cabinets when we need it?

For years I just could not understand it. I was extremely grateful and thankful for my blessings, but I could not understand why I deserved it, or why God chose to bless me. I found myself feeling guilty for being so blessed, when other people I knew were having so many difficulties in their lives. It just didn't seem fair for me to be blessed and happy, while others were dealt the hand of suffering and hardship.

It is so obvious that throughout these many years that I was living out of God's will and even through some of the years that I had gotten back into the church routine and loved God, I had become ignorant about God's amazing love. I had unknowingly allowed His hand to be removed from my life and didn't truly know or understand God's grace, nor His mercy. I knew *about* these things, had read *about* them in the Bible and heard sermons preached *about* His mercy, but I did not understand with my whole heart and therefore couldn't comprehend the infinite vastness of His grace. Fortunately, despite my inability to see through the clouds that blocked my view of understanding, God continued to pull me closer to Him through a series of events that impacted my life.

After becoming involved in our church for several years, I felt a calling on my heart to attend a women's ministry seminar that my church was offering in the year 2001. I was sure it would be an interesting topic. I was hungry for God's word and I hoped I might meet some new ladies and make a new friend. I had never been to one of these events before and I had no idea what the topic was. At the time, I also had no idea what God had in store for me, but He knew. Like a farmer would fertilize the soil to produce great fruit, God sent me to this seminar to fertilize my heart to produce fruits of the spirit. This seminar was the first sprinkling of fertilizer that God placed on my heart and was the day that my little rainbow finally started to sprout again. Similar to when God told Noah to sacrifice burnt offerings to Him, after he had saved him and his family from the flood, this was a defining moment for me. I was not expecting to have an encounter with God, but this would be the day in which God would clearly tell me to build him an alter and make my own sacrifices to him. Sacrifices such as privacy, pride, shame and embarrassment. Sacrifices that would allow me to use my sufferings to His glory.

Little did I know that this seminar was merely the beginning of a wonderful and powerful spiritual journey. Little did I know that it would result in many personal sacrifices eventually being offered up to God. Had I known that, I would probably have stayed home that day.

A New Shade of Yellow

Have you ever watched an old classic cartoon or Western where two rivals are fighting and one calls the other one a yellow-bellied scoundrel? Even in real life, yellow is not always a happy color, but can often be a symbol of fear and cowardliness.

The seminar started out with prayer and singing and nothing much out of the ordinary. The event speaker was from Proverbs 31 Ministries, based in Charlotte, North Carolina. Proverbs 31 is an organization whose mission is to touch women's hearts, build Godly homes and encourage them in their marriages and their roles as Christian mothers *(www.Proverbs31.org)*. As a result of this Proverbs 31 seminar, God would place the first of many permanent stitches into my broken heart and the recovery process would finally be able to begin. It turns out, as God so divinely planned it, that the Proverbs 31 speaker and president, Lysa TerKeurst, had been through an abortion when she was young and she was there to share her testimony of forgiveness and renewal.

Over the next hour, Lysa discussed in vivid detail the pain of what she had experienced as a result of her choice to have an abortion and the years she had hated herself for it. She also discussed how she had come to realize that God wanted to forgive her and all she had to do was ask. She explained in great detail how God had changed her life, forgiven her, provided peace and joy and mended her broken heart.

By the end of this hour-long testimony, it had taken every ounce of willpower and strength in my broken body and soul not to make a mad dash for the altar and throw myself onto it, sob out loud and beg God to forgive me. But I was just so broken inside that I couldn't move. I think I was also in shock, for this was the first time I had listened to someone else talk about the same horror that I had experienced, even though statistics state that one in every four women has been through that ordeal. Abortion is the silent killer of souls not to be mentioned, never to be discussed, all the while draining joy from each affected heart.

In an effort to avoid totally humiliating myself, and since my faith was not as strong as it needed to be at that time, I buried my feelings inside as I had done for so many years and just wept silently but fervently, all the while hoping that no one was paying any attention to me.

During this prayer time and amid my flood of tears, I pleaded with God for His divine mercy and grace, and, most importantly, for His forgiveness. I asked for His forgiveness over and over, in fact so many times that God was probably wondering if I had become a broken record instead of a broken soul. I had asked God for forgiveness before, but this time it was different. This time I actually believed that God had forgiven me. I believed with all my heart that He had heard my pleas and the sorrow and remorse for what I had done. I believed that I had repented and that God accepted my repentance. I believed, for the first time in 15 years, that my slate in heaven was wiped clean. Instantaneously, the heavy burden, the shame and the pain…were lifted, as if they had leapt from my heart, landed on a cloud and floated up to the heavens.

God had not delayed his forgiveness of my sin. He had forgiven me on that rainy, gloomy evening in June 1986 when I wept in my bed in the dark and begged for His forgiveness in the midst of my physical and emotional pain. All these years, it was I who had not forgiven myself. It was I, who as a result of my lack of faith and allowing myself to willfully fall from the light of God, could not believe God accepted me, loved me or was willing to forgive me.

I caused myself so many years of undue pain and suffering, and in turn caused others pain and suffering through my ungodly actions and behaviors, all as a result of not only my poor choices, but because I had convinced myself that God had not forgiven me, could not forgive me and would not forgive me. All these years, I had been doubting the one true God and His ability to forgive me. But once his forgiveness for my sin had sunk into my heart that day, I then asked for His forgiveness for my doubt and my lack of faith. Now I knew He had forgiven me 15 years ago, when I had first asked. If only back then I had opened my ears and my heart to hear the soothing words of mercy and love that He wanted to wash my soul with. If only then I had believed in His grace.

In that moment of redemption, I committed my life to Him once again. I brought new meaning to the term born-again Christian. I was born again—a new soul, a new heart, a new love for Christ and a new love for life. Most importantly, I had a new passion—for God. My heart was beating rapidly in my chest and overflowing with gratefulness and love.

In that same moment that my spirit was lifted and my heart quickened, I knew I was in the presence of God and my spiritual ears were suddenly opened for the first time in years. As a result, I clearly heard God's voice as if it had been announced over a loudspeaker. But,.I did not want to hear what He had to say. As I cowered in fear, He said, "Tracie, I have forgiven you. Will you share your testimony with others who need to hear of my grace, mercy and love?"

Instantly, I began telling God, practically in a screaming voice in my head, all the while still sobbing with tears, that I could never and would never tell anyone my most shameful secret and I certainly would never do it in a public setting. No, no, no! I believed I was forgiven; my gratefulness for His mercy was overwhelming, but not so overwhelming that I would tell anyone about the forgiven sin. I answered, "Oh, God, do not ask me to share my testimony…"but it was too late.

As soon as the doors of my heart were opened, my ears had been opened as well and I had heard God's voice loud and clear. I continued repeating in my head that I could never tell anyone, never. I realize now that obviously God was gently telling me at that time, in that very fragile moment of redemption and rebirth, that He wanted me to do exactly that. He had waited a long time for me to recognize His voice and His plan and he was not going to waste any time informing me of that plan.

Indeed, He was asking me to share my story with others and allow this painful experience to bring glory to His Kingdom. If this were not the case, why else would I have been having a heated argument with God over something that I had never even considered doing before, even in my wildest dreams (or nightmares)? Until this exact moment in time, I had never even forgiven myself, much less believed God had forgiven me. I had never spoken about the abortion with anyone since the day it had happened. I had never allowed myself to utter the word "abortion." So why would I even be entertaining the thought that I was going to have to tell anyone? Although God had been entertaining this thought for my entire life, I refused to entertain the thought myself. There was no way that I was going to find the key and let out the skeletons that I had secretly locked away in my heart forever.

NINE
Building the Ark

Genesis 6:14-16: *"So make yourself an ark of cypress wood;*
make rooms in it and coat it with pitch inside and out.
This is how you are to build it: The ark is to be 450 feet long,
75 feet wide and 45 feet high. Make a roof for it and
finish the ark to within 18 inches of the top. Put a door
in the side of the ark and make lower, middle and upper
decks. I am going to bring flood waters on the earth to
destroy all life under the heavens, every creature that
has the breath of life in it. Everything on earth will perish."

I am sure my feelings were similar to those that Noah must have
felt when God instructed him to build that enormous ship that would
take years to construct; to gather two of every creature on earth; and
the promise that he would escape a flood. He had no idea what a
flood was, since it had never rained on the earth before during the
entire 600 years that he had been alive!

I can envision Noah placing his hands over his ears and singing
"Mary had a Little Lamb," trying to drown out God's command that
sounded so utterly ridiculous and absurd. I can only imagine that
since Noah was merely human, just as you and I are, that he wished
that He had not heard God's command—but he did hear it and once
he had heard God's voice, it was too late to pretend that he hadn't
understood.

Remember what Noah did next? Genesis 6:22: *"Noah did everything just as God had commanded him."* We are told again about Noah's unyielding obedience in Genesis 7:5: *"And Noah did all that the Lord commanded him."* Noah obeyed! How I wish I had been as strong as Noah, but although the unconditional forgiveness and piercing peace I received during the seminar that day had affected my heart and life forever, I was not ready to move forward with God's plan for me. I was still in the recovery process of God's healing on my heart and my life. It would have been like having had major heart surgery and then going out the next day and trying to run a 10k marathon. Even though I had finally accepted that I was truly forgiven and felt God's peace on my heart regarding my sin, the pain, shame and the remorse was still in my memories and the thought of allowing this mistake to consume my life again was the last thing I was going to do.

I had heard God's voice and I'm positive he was saddened when he heard my response. Unlike Noah's, my response was quite the opposite....I bowed my head and quietly said, "No way, God. Forget it." I was a yellow-bellied scoundrel and ready to run for cover.

If you think you have heard God's voice, but what He is asking you to do seems insurmountable, then you should probably accept the fact that it was, indeed, God's voice. To confirm your suspicions, delve into God's word and look for confirmation as God leads you to specific passages. Pray and ask God for guidance and keep your spiritual eyes and ears open for messages that seem to reaffirm what you believe you have heard from God—for example, Bible verses that jump out at you and you feel compelled to glance back and read them again, messages from friends that mention that same subject, sermons or radio talk shows, etc.

Keep in mind that God doesn't give us easy tasks, but instead He will ask us to do things that can only be accomplished through His strength and supernatural power. I am not talking about physical strength; I am referring to emotional and spiritual strength. The only way that I can share my testimony, is because of the supernatural peace that God granted me and His strength and courage coursing through my veins every day as I try to pursue His will.

Lysa TerKeurst said it best in her book, titled *Radical Obedience*: "When God calls us to do something, most of the time we will not be able to do it in our own strength—either it is beyond our ability or beyond our natural human desire. It is not something we can strategize and manipulate into being in and of ourselves. It can only happen by God's divine intervention. The beauty of doing things beyond ourselves is that we will know it was by God's doing and His alone. And to Him we give all the glory."

If God asked us to do something easy, painless and without some type of sacrifice, would we really feel compelled to glorify Him after we accomplished the task? I think not. If we could quickly do what he asked, without any effort or sacrifice, it would be meaningless. So if God has spoken to you, not audibly, but through some or all of the ways that I just mentioned, then God is simply waiting for you to say *"yes."* You should take confidence in knowing that you may already have everything you need to succeed in whatever task he has set before you. If you have accepted Christ into your heart, He has already equipped your heart and soul with all the tools you will need to fulfill His purposes. It could be that he is just waiting for you to open the toolbox and start using the tools that he has given you to begin building your own ark, or "arcs." You have the power inside of you and if you don't feel that power and you continue to feel inadequate and incapable of fulfilling God's plan, then you are listening to the lies of Satan, instead of the truth of Christ.

Matthew 17:20 says, *"...because you have so little faith. I tell you the truth, if you have faith as small as a mustard seed, you can say to this mountain, 'Move from here to there' and it will move. Nothing will be impossible for you."*

Ephesians 3:20-21 says, *"Now to him who is able to do immeasurably more than all we ask or imagine, according to his power within us, to him be glory in the church, and in Christ Jesus throughout all generations, forever and ever! Amen."*

God is all the gas you need to get your spiritual motor revved up and running! Now go for the gusto!

TEN
The Covenant Promise

Genesis 9:8-11: *"Then God said to Noah and to his sons with him: I now establish my covenant with you and with your descendants after you and with every living creature that was with you........on earth. I establish my covenant with you. Never again will all life be cut off by the waters of a flood; never again will there be a flood to destroy the earth."*

Multiple Prisms of Color

After Noah obeyed God and fulfilled His commands, God secured Noah and his family safely in the ark and the let the full fury of the flood wreak havoc on the sinful world for forty days and nights. Before the flood occurred, this amazing story had been one of judgment on the sinful people of the world. But once Noah obeyed and the lives of he and his family were spared due to their righteousness, faith and obedience, the story blossoms into a tale of redemption and glory.

God promised Noah that He made a covenant with him. Genesis 9:8: *"Then God said to Noah and to his sons with him: I now establish my covenant with you and with your descendants after you and with every living creature that was with you—the birds, the livestock and all the wild animals, all those that came out of the ark with you—every living creature on earth."*

God's promise is solid, regardless of what we endure or whether or not we accept His truths. Just as he promised to protect Noah before and after the mighty flood, He has also promised to hold us in His loving care and protection. It may take some time to feel His arms around us, but the promise is always there.

God had allowed me the time to realize that although life is filled with storms and maybe even a few floods, that once we accept His grace and forgiveness, we can never be destroyed. When we accept Jesus as our risen savior, He becomes our spiritual life raft, which is strong enough to carry us through any storm, or flood, big or small.

The storms of life are what builds our faith, builds our character and builds our love for Him as we see His hand in ours during these hard times. Most importantly, when the flood waters rise, through our faith alone we are able to see that we are not drowning after all and that God will carry us to safety on His spiritual life raft, so that we can fulfill the purpose that He has ordained for our lives.

Noah's purpose after the great flood was to help replenish the earth with life, not just by his own offspring, but also by releasing the animals so that they could once again populate the land.

We are told of Noah's final task in Genesis 9:15-17: *"Then God said to Noah, 'Come out of the ark, you and your wife and your sons and their wives. Bring out every kind of living thing that is with you—the birds, the animals and all the creatures that move along the ground—so they can multiply on the earth and be fruitful and increase in number upon it.'"* And once again, Noah obeyed with a full heart. In fact, he and his family probably knocked each other down trying to get off of that boat after having spent many weeks afloat!! I feel confident Noah didn't hesitate on following that holy command to exit the boat!

Genesis 9:18-19: *"So Noah came out, together with his sons and his wife and his sons' wives. All the animals and all the creatures that move along the ground and all the birds—*

everything that moves on the earth—came out of the ark, one kind after another. " Noah knew without a doubt that God had spared him and loved him and that he would bless and protect his family as they prepared for their new life.

Even though many times we feel unworthy of God's love, we can remind ourselves that Noah was no different than people in today's society. He was just a working man with a family, with daily pressures and challenges, but He believed in God and God loved him and saved him from harm.

Genesis 8:1 says, *"But God remembered Noah and all the wild animals and the livestock that were with him in the ark and he sent a wind over the earth and the waters receded."* As a believer, nothing can separate us from our Lord and he never forgets about us. Just as God protected Noah, He will always be there to protect us as well.

Over the process of the next year following the life- changing seminar, Lysa's testimony stuck in my mind. I began reading many of her books and I followed the Proverbs 31 ministry closely. In fact, the daily email devotionals that I received each day from Proverbs 31 became one of God's primary mediums to speak directly to me. Who ever said that God couldn't send an email?! I cannot begin to tell you the dozens of times that God would speak to me through these daily email devotions. There were so many times in which I prayed fervent prayers about different concerns or situations in my life, only to shortly after receive an answer to that prayer, a suggestion for how to deal with that issue, or encouragement to carry me through that situation through the daily devotional email. There have been several times that I prayed about a very specific burden that I was carrying and within minutes, the devotion would appear in my email inbox and the topic would be so closely related to my prayer request, at times even using the exact words that I had used in my prayer, that tears would instantly fill my eyes. I do realize that telling you that I receive emails from God seems a bit crazy, but I also realize that this is one of the ways that God had chosen to speak to me. God has a specific way He wants to speak to each of his children. We just have to open our eyes and hearts to be on the lookout for the unique way He chooses to communicate to each of us as a unique and special person.

Despite my rejuvenated faith and love for the Lord and even during my continued following of Proverbs 31 Ministries, I experienced a period of time where I was struggling internally again. God had made it painfully apparent to me that He wanted me to share my testimony. His message was coming across loud and clear, over and over, as it seemed that every speaker, radio program host, songs, Bible verses, friends, TV shows, email devotions, sermons, you name it, were somehow telling me to step out in faith and follow my calling. The notion of simply irony went completely out the window! It got to the point that I was starting to think God was stalking me about this, because He just wouldn't let up! But I'm only human, was still a child in my faith, and still confused as to whether or not this actually was my calling. I certainly wouldn't want to humiliate and shame myself, my husband and my family, only to find out that I had misinterpreted what God's will was for my life. So I continued on with my life as normal and worked hard at strengthening my faith and my relationship with Jesus Christ, all the while knowing deep in my soul that I was being disobedient.

Two years later, in the fall of 2003, the women's ministry team at my church introduced another opportunity for Christian fellowship and faith building involving Beth Moore. Beth is such a powerful soldier in God's army. The Lord has gifted her with an amazing talent of speaking and preaching, the gift of understanding and delivering his message to others, and the gift of bringing countless thousands of women to know Christ. Her Bible studies have brought great strength to me and greatly increased my fellowship with my Lord.

This next women's ministry fellowship opportunity was to actually see Beth Moore in person in Richmond, Virginia. I was so excited to get to see her in the flesh! I expected to be honored to be in the same building with the famous Beth Moore of whom I admired greatly, not for who she was, but for what she had allowed God to do through her. I expected to have a great time, to learn more about God, spend time with friends and to increase my spiritual walk with Christ. What I was not expecting was to be so profoundly moved, so emotionally torn by her message, or so enthralled with being in the presence of over 15,000 women worshiping God that I would be brought to my knees. I was not expecting yet another encounter with God. And I certainly didn't expect it to change my life.

I sat through the two-day Beth Moore seminar in awe. Surely her message was meant for me alone. She so awesomely made it clear that we are to take our experiences and painful situations and begin using them for God's glory and that when we do that, we actually become a threat to Satan and help build God's kingdom. I soon realized that Beth Moore was just like me, a broken soul who had experienced many trials and sufferings, but who had the courage to use them to God's glory. I have no doubt that it is painful and somewhat embarrassing for her to tell the world of her abuse as a child and the hardships she endured, but she didn't let that stop her from following God's command. I realized that the only real difference between Beth Moore and myself was that she had allowed God to use her. Years ago, Beth had acknowledged and accepted God's call on her life and she had been willing to take the next step to allow Him to use her for his glory.

As I intently listened to Beth's messages, they sounded vaguely familiar to the message I had heard two years earlier from Lysa TerKeurst. (Okay, I admit, I knew it wasn't ironic that Beth's message was the same topic when she could have chosen any topic to speak on that day!). But, oh, how I wanted to be a threat to Satan now! I wanted so badly to take revenge on him, not only for how he had afflicted my heart and my life, but also for how he had infiltrated my mind years ago to coerce me into believing that his way was the right way. I wanted to get him back for luring me away from righteousness at a young age, for all the horrible things he placed in my path, for all the temptations that I had succumbed to and as a result for the wrong choices that I had made.

God was using Beth to speak to me—forget about those other 15,000-plus women who were also there. God had placed Tracie Miles there, in that place, at that exact time in her life, so that He could speak to her through Beth Moore, just as he had done with Lysa TerKeurst. I knew that God had led Beth to preach that specific message that day, just because I, a little ol' unimportant, shameful and broken sinner, would be there listening with a hurting heart and a soul that yearned for healing.

This event was merely another blatant confirmation that God so desired for me to move forward with helping Him build His kingdom. I had not misinterpreted God's will for my life. I had merely once again refused to open my eyes and my heart to see all the signs that He was giving me. But here were His words again, the all-too-familiar call to follow Him, in my face, clear as a bell.

After Beth's message was delivered, this powerful congregation of women sang a praise hymn that you may be familiar with, which has a chorus which repeats, "Yes Lord, yes Lord, yes, yes Lord." I knew in my heart that it was time to surrender. It was time to surrender my pride, surrender my ego, surrender my shame and follow Him. As always, God knew the status of my heart at that very moment in time, so this was a perfect time for him to call out to me again. I clearly heard his voice echoing in my head, the familiar words I had heard before, *"Tracie, now will you follow me and share your testimony with others?"*

I knew the extent of how much these two testimonies I had heard in the last couple years had changed and affected my salvation and my life and I suddenly felt a compelling obligation that maybe I should consider the lives that might be changed as a result of hearing my testimony and telling people how God forgave me and healed my heart and soul. I so badly wanted to lift my hands to the heavens and yell out loud the words "YES LORD!" I thought to myself that if only one person's heart could be touched, if one person drew closer to Jesus, or if one person accepted Jesus into their heart as a result of hearing my testimony, it would all be worth it. If only one young girl who was considering abortion and who was lost and didn't know what to do would hear about my poor choices, my pain and the years it took to restore my heart and then choose pro-life over pro-choice, it would all be worth it.

For the first time I found myself desperately yearning to say, "Okay, God, I will follow you." I knew it was time, so did I follow Noah's example of obedience? Regrettably, I did not. I still did not obey. Can you believe it? I was still so afraid. Still so fearful of what my family and friends and church members would think of me. What if they rejected me? What if they whispered about me when I walked by? What if they pointed at me? What if they thought that I was a terrible person and most certainly unworthy of serving God through our church anymore? How could I live my life knowing that people were talking about me behind closed doors?

The shame and crushing fear of rejection began pouring over me as relentlessly as the flood waters that poured from the sky onto the sinful, unrighteous people whom Noah had left behind. This fear completely overpowered me and thus overpowered my willingness to follow God's command. I just could not let myself give in.

In addition, there was one other thought that was ripping at my heartstrings. I could not bear thinking about the sorrow and pain that I would surely cause my family. My family never knew about the abortion and I knew that telling them would hurt them deeply. My heart broke into millions of pieces as I could already envision my mother weeping, not only for what I had done, but also for what I had endured. I knew her heart would break for me. The last thing I wanted to do was to hurt her, my father, or my in-laws by telling them about what had occurred so many years ago. I also didn't want to hurt or embarrass my husband. But finally something occurred to me after much prayer and pleading with God for answers... *"Wasn't true faith all about endurance?"* Yes, I had endured terrible heartbreak and pain. Yes, I had suffered years of unfortunate consequences as a result my poor choices, but I had come out on top and was righteous in God's eyes because I was forgiven.

Psalms 130:3-4 tells us this: *"If you, Oh Lord kept a record of my sins, O Lord, who could stand? But with you there is forgiveness; therefore you are feared."* God not only has the power to forgive, but He holds the ability to forget. Unlike our human hearts, He wasn't keeping a record of my sin, so why should I? God had forgiven me and forgotten my sins.

I came to the realization that I needed to quit beating myself up about my past and prepare myself to endure whatever God had planned for my life. I had to mentally, emotionally and spiritually prepare myself to endure anything that the future would hold. I had to rely solely on my faith. I realized it was time to sow endurance if I wanted to reap my heavenly harvest.

I was reminded of what Jesus had to endure on the cross so that I and all other sinners of the world, could have eternal life. Jesus endured unimaginable and inhumane suffering, not only in his physical body, but also in his human heart. He knew that dying on the cross would bring his mother, Mary, unbearable pain, as she sat at the foot of the cross weeping for her broken and bleeding son. I feel sure that Mary would have traded places with Jesus in a heartbeat, so that her precious son would not have to suffer, just as I know my mother would have wanted to do for me had I told her about my unplanned pregnancy when it occurred.

It has been said many times that Jesus actually died of a broken heart, when the sword that pierced His side also pierced His heart.

But despite knowing that his eventual death would break hearts on earth, including the hearts of his own family members whom He dearly loved, Jesus exhibited incredible endurance, not only on the cross, but also throughout His entire life and all for the glory of His Father's kingdom. He expects us to do the same. As believers, we are expected to exhibit that same faithful endurance and He promises to walk beside us, holding our hand and leading us to a path of freedom.

I also needed to ask God to remove all of these fears from my heart. Isaiah 41:10 tells us how to put these fears aside, *"So do not fear, for I am with you; do not be dismayed, for I am your God; I will strengthen you and help you with my righteous hand."* But getting rid of our human fears is a lot easier said than done. It's one thing to ask God to take away the fear, but it's another thing to actually allow him to take total control over our human emotions.

As I continued to hover in the shadow of fear and immerse myself in a cloud of concern for those I loved most, the result of my disobedience only made things worse. Now I not only was ashamed of my past mistakes, but I was ashamed of myself and my outright refusal to follow God's command. I was ashamed that I wasn't being more faithful and that I kept allowing fear to creep into my soul.

I knew God was disappointed in me...again. I continued to torture myself by repeatedly thinking negative and damaging thoughts, such as, "What is wrong with me? Why can't I just have more faith and believe that He is in control? Why can't I trust that God will prevail and that everything will be okay, maybe even better than okay? Why can't I accept the belief that if I am doing God's will, that He will provide for me and protect me? Why can't I be a better Christian? I am such a terrible example of a believer. I know God is going to give up on me. I'm such a disappointment to Him. I am so ridiculously unworthy to serve a holy, pure and righteous God." As this self-induced emotional abuse suffocated my heart, I gave Satan yet another opportunity to quell my willingness to step forward. So, you guessed it—once again, I stayed glued to my auditorium seat, trying to wipe away my tears, all the while hurting and consumed with remorse for my disobedience and lack of faith.

A Tapestry of Colors Begins to Appear

In the secular corporate position that I held for seven years, which is where I was employed during God's calling on my life which I continually disregarded, I was required to do a lot of business travel. Although the disadvantages of traveling far outweigh the advantages, God used the time I spent on airplanes to draw me closer and closer to Him. Isn't it amazing how God works? At each airport I would purchase a Christian motivational or devotional book that I would have otherwise not purchased, just so I would have something to occupy my time. I have read so many wonderful books as a result and God has used these Christian books to educate me and mold me. I also began carrying my Bible with me on trips, which increased the amount of time I actually spent in His word. The frequent travel, although it caused challenges for my family, allowed me to have rare opportunities to have some real quiet time…meaningful quiet time, all alone, just me and God. And as a housewife, employee, wife and mother of three, any quiet time at all was a sheer miracle!

There is just something so special about air travel and being above the clouds with the blinding sunshine and the warmth of its closeness warming your face that makes you feel close to God. It is easy to imagine how beautiful and peaceful heaven must be, as you soar above the breathtaking clouds and seem closer to the God who created everything than you could ever feel on the ground.

The world is so peaceful above the clouds. You can quickly forget all your worries when all you can see is miles of fluffy white cotton, blue skies, subtle pink and yellow highlights and yellow sunshine. But on some days, as soon as the plane dipped beneath the clouds to make our descent, I realized that the day wasn't as I had thought at all. It was dreary, clouds were black and not white, and it was raining and gloomy. I instantly felt saddened and wanted to leap back up where the beauty had brought joy into my heart, where I was close to the heavens, where peace was so easily obtained.

During this descent into gloominess, God gently spoke to my heart. God wants us to feel close to him and bask in the warmth of His peace every day. The only requirement is that we turn our faces towards Him so we can feel his warmth. We do not need to be 30,000 feet in the air to feel like He is near. He is as close as we want him to be and that we will allow Him to be, every second of every day. When we are faced with trials, we should seek God's guidance and rise above the problems through his strength, grace and mercy, so that we can once again bask in peacefulness. Just as I wanted to rise back up into the clouds back into the peacefulness, that is what He wants for us to do every day.

On one particular business trip in late 2003, as I settled into this peacefulness in the air feeling close to my Lord, I began reading another book from Lysa TerKeurst, titled *Living Life on Purpose*. This book was again about her testimony of faith, her abortion and how she had overcome her fears and used her painful experiences to help others come to know Christ and to ultimately fulfill God's purpose for her life. It was a typical plane ride and I sat peacefully reading while crowded against the airplane window, hoping that the flight would be smooth and that the person sitting next to me would not try to talk to me.

As I continued to read the book, looking for purpose in my life, I came across a profound sentence that Lysa had written regarding her willingness to sacrifice her pride and use her testimony as a powerful tool for spreading God's truth. Lysa stated that sharing her testimony has had many purposes, including helping her heart to heal, discovering her purpose in life and being instrumental in preventing other young girls from terminating their pregnancies. But it was her final comment that jumped off the page and landed right on my heart. She wrote the following simple, yet life-transforming statement…*"I now know that my child's life was not for nothing."*

The very moment I read that sentence, it felt as if someone had hit me in the stomach. I felt as if the wind had been knocked out of me. I actually physically felt the sensation of being punched in the gut. I almost choked and then caught my breath so quickly that the person in the seat beside me looked over to see if I was okay. I had a lump in my throat and tears poured down my face. The Holy Spirit had spoken, in my heart, in my head, in my soul—and my body had felt it. I no longer had to worry about the person next to me wanting to strike up a conversation, because after this episode they probably wanted to change seats!

What I came to realize through that experience and that simple statement is, that the truth is I can never bring back the child I gave up, but the very least I can do is use that experience to teach others not to make the same mistake and help to convince them to turn to the Lord our God for everything. The least I can do is be willing to take the next step, for God and for my lost child. I wanted my lost child's life to have a purpose. I could use my testimony to show others that with God's awesome grace and mercy, we can triumph over Satan's bondage from painful sins of our past, and that no matter how bad the sin, God so desires to forgive us and use us, His precious children, to bring glory to Him. I can use this experience to possibly help young girls who are considering abortion, to choose life over death, to choose God over Satan and to choose an abundant life over the bondage of sin. I can be a positive witness to teach the value of abstinence and the sacredness of virginity until marriage. I can help young people understand that even if they have chosen not to maintain their virginity, that God not only forgives them, but can make them spiritually pure again.

I realize now that God will go to any lengths to get His message across and when He speaks, we are faithfully and lovingly obligated to listen.

ELEVEN
The Promise of a Rainbow

Genesis 9:16: *"Whenever the rainbow appears in the clouds, I will see it and remember the everlasting covenant between God and all living creatures of every kind on the earth. So God said to Noah, 'This is the sign of the covenant I have established between me and all life on the earth.'"*

The Colors Begin Taking Their Places in the "Arc"

This past year had been one of great understanding and revelation for me, and so God decided to exercise his sense of humor and end the year off with a bang!

In December 2003, the Holy Spirit spoke to me again, in such a way that I physically felt His presence, just as I had on that unforgettable day in the airplane. I had felt God calling me to join the Women's Ministry team the prior year and therefore had become an active member of that team for the previous twelve months. Following God on that command was an easy one, since it didn't cause me any pain, suffering, or embarrassment. It really didn't require me to make any real sacrifices, just a little bit of time to attend meetings and help with events. I loved event planning and fellowshipping with other women, so this seemed liked a great way to serve Christ... but then God tossed a kink into the plan.

One evening after church, I was leisurely chatting with the current women's ministry director. I learned she would soon be resigning to pursue other ministry opportunities. We talked for a while and she mentioned that God had placed someone on her heart to take over the role of women's ministry director and she would continue to pray about it. I said I would do the same. Once again, another encounter with God was not on my agenda for that day.

As I drove home that evening, a familiar sensation washed over me. I was out of breath and my heart was beating rapidly. It was similar to the feeling I had experienced on the plane a few months earlier, of taking a blow to the stomach, but fortunately since I was driving at 55 mph, it was a much softer blow. I made it home safely and tried to watch TV for a while and get my mind on something else, but the feeling of the presence of the Holy Spirit would not go away. God had something to say and He wanted me to listen.

I tossed and turned all night and did not get a restful night's sleep. So the next morning I prayed to God to ask Him what His will was for me, but also I needed to let him know a few things first. Was He calling me to lead the women's ministry for this large church? If so, I needed to "nip that idea in the bud," as Barney Fife would say! I would be the first to say that was a ridiculous idea. When I told my husband and family of this potential opportunity that I was contemplating, they were all shocked that I would even consider taking on more responsibility for anything. Had all the current stress in my life made me lose some brain wave activity?

I had a full-time job, which kept me extremely busy, traveling extensively and seriously stressed out. I was absolutely living in a state of commitment overload. I had a husband to care for. I had three small children who were not only physically and emotionally needy, but had dance lessons, t-ball practice, choir practice, church activities, cheerleading, soccer, piano, school and homework. I had a house that needed cleaning. I had loads of clothes to wash, fold, dry and put away. Blah Blah Blah. The excuses rambled on and on, but I will spare you the rest of them.

However, deep inside my heart, I knew that my primary excuse was this—*I was unworthy*. I was a sinner. I had scary skeletons in my closet of life. I was not a Bible scholar, nor a professor of theology. I didn't spend my daily quiet time with God as I should. I had not even read the whole Bible in its entirety! I couldn't quote that many Bible verses, nor had I ever been open with sharing my faith in the past. I never prayed aloud and I had never led anyone to Christ except my own children. I had not been through an evangelism class. To put it bluntly, my spiritual resume was not very impressive. So why would God call me to do this? I began to tell God, in my oh-so-intelligent voice, "Lord, please listen to me. I am not qualified, surely you meant to call someone else for this and you just made a tiny mistake by asking me! Or maybe I just misunderstood your command or heard you wrong. Whatever the reason, the answer is no."

My insecurities were marching full force ahead, with Satan happily leading the way. My myriad of excuses seemed very valid in my mind and even the slightest consideration of taking on such a huge commitment, knowing that I was already stretched thin, was the farthest thing from my mind. I continued to try to forget about the Holy Spirit's nudging and since I had been practicing the art of ignoring God's call for years, I thought I could easily push it out of my mind and move on.

But it wasn't the farthest thing from God's mind and He most certainly was not pushing it aside. So the next morning, just to get God off my back, I decided it couldn't hurt to just casually inquire about how much time was actually devoted to heading up this ministry. Maybe I could squeeze in a few hours here and there occasionally for God's work. So I sent off a one-sentence email to the current director and just asked that one simple question about the time commitment.

After the current director had answered that question and several other follow-up questions and after I shared with her my potential interest a few days later, she confided in me that it was my name that God had placed on her heart all these weeks as someone who could take over leadership of this ministry, even though she thought it was a farfetched idea, knowing the details of how busy my life already was. I was honored and surprised and both of us were thrilled to see God's plan unfolding right before our eyes. But still, I was reluctant. I was fearful of taking more time away from my family and not being able to handle the pressures of both my corporate position and my ministry responsibilities. But through prayer and faith, I pushed those fears aside and allowed God to take me by the hand like a little lost child and begin leading the way.

As you would suspect, God worked it all out. Imagine that! Looking back, it is difficult for me to understand how I got everything done. Satan had tried every trick in the book to make this time difficult for my family and me and to convince me that I had made yet another wrong decision. He did his best to coerce me into believing that I did not have time to serve God in this capacity and he would continually feed on my fears of over-commitment.

The months leading up to this decision had been very difficult, with a demanding job, excessive travel, ridiculous deadlines, time-consuming projects, obligations for the children and their schools, my husband working very long hours, a family member experiencing the loss of a baby and a heartbreaking illness…how could I consider taking on anything else? Had I lost my mind completely?

Some friends and even family members actually thought I had lost my mind, for they knew how busy and chaotic my life already was. Taking on any other commitments was basically emotional suicide. But I knew God had called me and I just couldn't let Him down again. Surely I can at least follow this one simple command.

Jeremiah 29: 11 says, *" 'For I know the plans I have for you,' declares the Lord, plans to prosper you and not harm you, plans to give you hope and a future."* This verse from Jeremiah was literally haunting me. It had come up so many times over the prior months and years that it was starting to get a little creepy. Every time I turned around, there was that verse again. God had not only been stalking me, but it was as if He had created a blinking neon sign that popped up everywhere I went that read "Hey, I have a plan for you! Get with the program! Jeremiah 29:11!"

I finally fell to my knees, begged for forgiveness for my lack of faith and disobedience and gave in to God. I knew He had plans for me and I knew He wanted to prosper me, so finally I conceded. Finally, after years of procrastination, without hesitation, but with some internal reservations, I fully committed to do His work.

God tells us throughout His word that He will be our strength when we need it. Two examples of this promise can be found in Psalm 29:11: *"The Lord gives strength to his people; the Lord blesses his people with peace"* and in Psalm 105:4: *"Look to the Lord and his strength; seek his face always."*

If we commit our lives and our time to Him, He will be the provider of the strength we need. He will allow time to stand still when we need it to and He will show us the way to do things that we think are impossible. How silly to think God would call us to a purpose, but would not be there to help us fulfill that purpose.

Romans 12:2 tells us this: *"Do not conform any longer to the pattern of this world, but be transformed by the renewing of your mind. Then you will be able to test and approve what God's will is—his good, pleasing and perfect will."*

God was not merely making his will known to me, but also wanted to me understand that He would prevail and he would give me the strength and the time needed to fulfill his wishes. I knew I needed to transform my mind if I wanted God to transform my life and my circumstances. He was not merely helping me with my time constraints during this time of leadership, but he was again adding more sunlight to my rainbow, which by the way, had finally started to glow with hints of vivid colors. He was using each stepping stone of my life to further prepare me for the ultimate work that He had in store for me. Each stone helping to construct that glorious bridge that was to be my ticket to true freedom. This ministry opportunity had led me to begin building a true relationship with my Father—a relationship from the core of my being.

The Rainbow Within Reach

God was getting impatient. When God calls one of His children to do something, He expects obedience. We are told in 1 Peter 3:19-20 *"Through whom also he went and preached to the spirits in prison who disobeyed long ago when God waited patiently in the days of Noah while the ark was being built."* God is patient, but He also expects us to do His will eventually. Noah took a very long time to build the ark, but at least God could see that Noah was making progress. The only thing God could see me doing was treading water! God is a loving and patient God, nurturing and teaching all along the way, but the time comes when God expects an answer and grows weary of waiting for us to obey.

During this time of disobedience, although I still did not feel I was emotionally ready to move forward in service and share my testimony, I experienced many trials. My job had become even more demanding; the business traveling increased, which put even more strains on my family. My mommy-guilt was at an all-time high as I had to travel more and more away from my children. The people I worked for were very unappreciative of my efforts and I received little recognition, thus it was very unrewarding; I was constantly criticized by my superiors to such a harsh degree that I had lost my own self-confidence and had begun to feel incompetent and incapable of doing anything right. I began to become very insecure and wore my feelings on my sleeve at work and at home. To top it off, my immediate and extended family experienced various difficulties with illnesses and even death. It seemed that things just kept getting worse and worse. I didn't understand why my life had seemed to turn upside down and I was being stalked by hardships.

Looking back I can see that God was allowing me to endure these trials in an effort to help me "wake up and smell the coffee." I was NOT obeying his command. I was not striving to become the woman that I knew I could be. I believe that He was tired of waiting. He was tired of relentlessly trying to make His will known to me. Just because *I* did not think I was ready, did not mean that God would let me off the hook. It was not my decision, it was His decision. It was not my story that needed to be shared, it was HIS STORY. He had ordained a plan for my life and the time had come for me to carry out that plan. Although He had used the past few years to help prepare me for my journey, He needed to let me know that He was ready for me to obey. There is a time for everything and the time had come to surrender to obedience. I was broken. I was desperate. I was ready to listen. Thus, once again, the doors were opened for God to come in.

First Peter 2:8 says: *"...and, a stone that causes men to stumble and a rock that makes them fall. They stumble because they disobey the message—which is also what they were destined for."*

The stones that had caused me to stumble in life were the very ones that were also building my character and my destiny. I was being disobedient by not following God's command and was stumbling head over heels to a destiny of problems, trials and life away from God. Satan was having another big party at my expense and I did not like it! So far the devil had been successful in making me stumble and keeping me from surrendering to God's will, by consuming me with low self-esteem and feelings of rejection and lack of worth. But I finally realized that if I didn't act soon, God might give up on me and give someone else the opportunity for service and witnessing that He had tried to give to me! I did need to wake up and smell the coffee—but it wasn't just any old coffee, it was a huge cup of Starbucks—the best there is! As painful as it was going be to bare my soul, share my mistakes and my sins with the world, swallow my pride and put God first, I knew it was what God expected of me…and it was time. I was horrified to think that God would call someone else to carry out the plan that He had originally intended to use me for!

I prayed for weeks for God to fill me with His spirit, to fill me with the reassurance that only He could provide and to fill my mind with the knowledge to know what steps I should be taking to fulfill his command and in turn experience the fullness of life that He had planned for me. And do not doubt for a moment that Jeremiah 29:11 "ironically" continued to pop up time and time again and continued to be my little lantern of guiding light along my path to self-discovery.

Touching the Rainbow

Shortly after attending the seminar in 2003, my emotions had been overflowing. God had led me at that time to begin putting my thoughts on paper, and so I started writing a book…this book. But as my fear and lack of faith hindered all God's efforts to push me into a life of service for Him, I had left my story on my hard drive for over two years. In my third year of being involved with women's ministry, I finally heeded God's call to complete the story.

There was no special event that occurred, nor another moving seminar that pushed me to the point of action. It was purely a matter of the heart. I had now to come to expect encounters with God and yearned for them daily. It is so exciting to always be on the lookout for God and be ready to experience his amazing wonders.

My heart was again aching and yearning, but this time the ache was not because of a past sin, but because of disobedience. Again and again, Jeremiah 29:11 resounded in my head, *"For I know the plans I have for you; Plans to prosper and not harm you, plans to give you hope and a future."* I finally made the final determination that I desperately wanted what God had in store for me, whatever it was! I was sure it was something wonderful, since God had been relentless about putting that verse into my consciousness and in my face! I had gradually developed an extraordinary hunger to be showered with blessings that I could not fathom and to enjoy the prosperous life and abundant joy that awaited me.

I had a burning desire to help those who were lost and hurting come to know Christ. I wanted to help little babies be saved from death in the womb and given an opportunity for life. I longed for all of this deeply in my soul and especially since my soul was now filled with sunshine and many beautiful rainbows. I wanted to share those rainbows with others. I wanted to help other people discover their rainbows in Christ just as I had done! Thus, I dusted off my computer, pulled up my original manuscript and let my fingers do the walking, but this time my heart was doing the talking. I was not just recording facts or personal memoirs; I was allowing my fingers to be the instrument for God to write His story.

I studied my Bible diligently, always looking for guidance, searching for confirmation and praying for strength through His word. I prayed that God would help the words to flow from my fingertips like water flows over a waterfall, with each drop of water making a tiny difference in the whole body of water below it.

One rainy Saturday evening, as I had my brain working overtime on my writing, my thoughts suddenly came to a standstill. I guess you could say I had a writer's block. Instead of focusing on what God was leading me to say, I was unexpectedly engulfed with thoughts of rejection and fear. It was as if all of my fears came pouring down on me and drenched me with the shame and fear of rejection that I had held onto for so long. My face felt hot and my heart rate had increased. I suddenly felt like the people must have felt in Noah's time, when they were drowning in the flood but unable to find safety on the ark.

For a brief moment, the flood had returned and I needed to find safety once again in God's arms. I began to think to myself, *Maybe this was all a big mistake? How can I really know that what I think that God has called me to do is in deed my calling? Maybe I can't come up with the words to write because God is giving me a sign that He doesn't really want me to share my testimony after all?* Now isn't that wishful thinking! But I quickly took control of my emotions and realized that it was just Satan acting up again. Satan was endlessly trying to fill my head with doubts, insecurities, rejection and the fear of the unknown future. I was now becoming a threat to him and he wanted to put a stop to it by feeding on the things that he knew would make me stumble. And take my word for it, I was stumbling head over heels again, just as Satan had predicted.

I bowed my head and immediately began praying that God would allow me to continue to pursue His will, to overcome the attacks of Satan on my heart and oh, by the way, would He mind confirming, just one last time, what His will was for me? I just wanted one more example of proof that God was ready for me to move ahead. Just one more little sign, God? Please?

There is no doubt in my mind that God was scratching his head with confusion and had begun to believe that I had some form of attention deficit syndrome or amnesia at this point. How many obvious signs had I already received from Him? Did He have to catch my lawn shrubbery on fire for me to actually believe His words?

That Saturday evening, I had prayed my life's theme verse again, Jeremiah 29:11, and God quietly revealed to me that I should read on. So I read Jeremiah 29:12-13 and it says, *"Then you will call upon me and come and pray to me and I will listen to you. You will seek me and find me when you seek me with all your heart.*

I will be found by you, declares the Lord and will bring you back from captivity..."

Yes, He had heard my prayer. And regardless of the number of times that God had given me tangible and intangible evidence that He had heard my prayers, each and every time another prayer is so obviously and divinely answered, it never fails to bring me to tears and fill my heart with joy. He knew that I was still being held captive, still tangled in the bondage of shame and feelings of unworthiness, although the reins had been loosened on Satan's grasp. He wrapped His loving arms around me and soothed me through His word. All I had to do was seek Him with all my heart and He would hear me.

The following day, after I had embarrassingly once again asked for God's confirmation of His will for my life, I slumped out of bed on that rainy Sunday morning, begrudgingly got everyone dressed in their Sunday best, and went to church with my husband and children. I have to admit that I did consider staying at home on that muggy, gloomy, rainy day, but my heart convinced me otherwise. I scrambled to get all the children out the door and ran through the rain to the car.

As God so miraculously planned it, the pastor's sermon was about a most interesting and relevant topic—procrastination. Of all people, I could probably win a Nobel Peace Prize for procrastination! I had spent years mastering that not-so-wonderful personality trait!

The moment that I heard what the sermon topic was about, my eyes, ears and heart perked up. I sat straight up in my pew and anxiously waited to hear God speak to me. I knew God had a very special message for me that morning. I knew another holy encounter was around the bend. I also knew, that despite my endless excuses for not following His commands, that it all boiled down to one thing—procrastination.

As my pastor so eloquently put it, procrastination is the barrier to seeing God at work in our lives and by procrastinating, we miss out on the joy and abundant life that God wants us to have. It may be perfectly justified in our minds to say, "I'll do it later God, when *I* am ready," but God does not accept that as a valid excuse. He is not a God of excuses; He is a God of action and obedience.

Deuteronomy 1:6 says, as the Lord was speaking to Moses, " *The Lord God said to us at Horeb, You have stayed long enough at this mountain. Break camp and advance into the hill country of the Amorites; go to all the neighboring peoples in the Arabah, in the mountains, in the western foothills, in the Negev and along the coast, to the land of Canaanites and to Lebanon, as far as the great river, the Euphrates. See, I have given you this land. Go in and take possession of the land that the Lord swore he would give to your fathers—to Abraham, Isaac and Jacob— and to their descendants after them.* "

Even though God made promises to Moses about the promised land, had taken care of the needs of the people throughout the entire journey; even though Moses knew He was the one and only Heavenly Father who had already provided multiple miracles in His presence, including parting the Red Sea for goodness sakes, Moses hesitated and doubted to enter the promised land. Don't you sometimes have the urge to knock on the skull of Moses and say, "Hello? Is anyone there? Are the lights on, but nobody is home?"

When reading this biblical story of Moses, I find myself pondering, "What in the world was Moses thinking?!." How could Moses not listen to God's command and heed His words? How could he have so little faith in the promise that God made to him? But that is just what Moses did and it is what we all do when we waste time, listen to other people's complaints which shake our confidence, allow fear to set in and ultimately allow a lack of faith to take control of our mind. Procrastination turns us right back into that yellow-bellied scoundrel! God was telling me that morning that I had stayed long enough on my mountain of safety, it was time for me to break camp and move forward into the promised land.

I had to learn the hard way that a lack of obedience has many consequences and will cause a domino effect of problems. When God commands us to do something and we don't act on that command immediately, or at a minimum eventually, Satan is given a powerful threshold to prevent us from acting at all. If we allow him to latch onto that threshold too tightly, we lose sight of our promised land and the possibility exists that God will take away the opportunity to enter the promised land and oh what a loss we will experience.

Time also allows for fear to set in and fear is the most powerful of all emotions. The more time I spent deciding whether or not I should share my testimony, the more time that Satan had to adamantly convince me that I could not endure the imminent rejection, judgment and shame of my sin coming to light. How could I possibly think that God could use me? I'm just a nobody. I'm a sinner. I'm not anywhere as wonderful, spiritually gifted or godly as Billy Graham, Anne Graham Lotz, Beth Moore, or Lysa TerKeurst, or any other Christian in this world for that matter. But as I gradually allowed God to work on my heart and slowly break down that wall of fear, He revealed a wonderful verse to me. Proverbs 14:9 reads, *" Fools mock at making amends for sin, but goodwill is found among the upright. "*

The truth is that there probably will be people who will mock me for my sin and judge me mercilessly, but I finally came to a place where I knew I could live with that. I knew that I could stand upright, with my head held high, with God standing firmly beside me as my biggest supporter.

This was reaffirmed in my heart when I came across another beautiful verse in Psalm 18:18, *"They confronted me in the day of my disaster, but the Lord was my support. "*

I also read the verses in Peter 3:13-17 which tell us, *"Who is going to harm you if you are eager to do good? But even if you should suffer for what is right, you are blessed. Do not fear what they fear, do not be frightened. But in your hearts set apart Christ as Lord. Always be prepared to give an answer to everyone who asks you to give the reason for the hope that you have. But do this with gentleness and respect, keeping a clear conscious, so that those who speak maliciously against your good behavior in Christ may be ashamed of their slander. "*

Now listen to how The Message Bible interprets this same passage in Psalms: *"If with heart and soul you're doing good, do you think you can be stopped? Even if you suffer for it, you're still better off. Don't give the opposition a second thought. Through thick and thin, keep your hearts up and tell anyone who asks why you're living the way you are and always with the utmost courtesy. Keep a clear conscience before God so that when people throw mud at you, none of it will stick. They'll end up realizing that they're the ones who need a bath. It's better to suffer for doing good, if that's what God wants, than to be punished for doing bad. "*

Wow! If this interpretation doesn't make it abundantly clear that following God's command is the right path to take, I don't know what will! Even if I do have to endure some embarrassment, criticism and pain, I can have faith knowing that God will deal with them and that I need to let their words just go in one ear and out the other and without ever landing on my heart. I realized that I could not let the fear of other people's opinions rule my life. I also had to recognize that the people who may turn against me or criticize me would eventually have to face judgement themselves. It was not up to me to worry about their behavior or let it stand in the way of what God had planned for my life. With God in my fan club, how can I go wrong? Isn't God's Word wonderful?!

Have you ever had a problem that you were dealing with that kept you awake? You lay in bed late at night in the dark and quiet, thinking and worrying about it, and suddenly the problem seemed to grow from a little pebble in your shoe to a huge boulder ready to crush you like an ant? However, in the morning, as you go about your day and ponder the same problem again, that problem does not seem quite so overwhelming?

That is what happens with procrastination. The more we procrastinate to follow our heart and obey God's commands, the bigger our fear seems to become. Whatever we choose to focus on is what will begin to grow in our hearts. For example, if we focus on our problems and insecurities, they will soon become that big boulder waiting to crush us. However, if we choose to focus on Jesus, He will become the rock of our salvation and that rock will crush those fears and insecurities, not our hearts and souls. Jesus says to us in John 16:33, *"I have told you these things, so that in me you may have peace. In this world you will have trouble. But take heart! I have overcome the world."* Our Lord has overcome the world! What fools we are to think that He is incapable of overcoming our small issues?

The worst consequence of procrastination and a delayed obedience for God's command is that we miss out on what God has in store for us and we are unable to enjoy fullness of life that he intends for us. What a shame that we should miss out on incredible blessings, all as a result of allowing Satan to convince us that our procrastination, or in other words, our blatant disobedience, is fully justified. Obedience is not optional with God. What if Noah had procrastinated on building the ark? Do you think God would have said, "Oh, that's too bad, I guess I'll have to think of another way to destroy all mankind." Nope, He eventually would have found someone else to carry out His will and Noah would have been left to endure the rising waters. You can consider the analogy we have all heard of either "sink or swim." We can either refuse to obey and sink to the bottom of that slimy pit waiting to engulf us, or follow God's call and swim to that spiritual life raft I mentioned earlier. He leaves it up to us!

From Genesis 15:1: *"Do not be afraid, Abram. I am your shield, your very great reward,"* where God tells us that he will protect us through anything, to Revelations 22:12: *"Behold, I am coming soon! My reward is with me and I will give to everyone according to what he has done. I am the Alpha and Omega, the First and the Last, the Beginning and the End,"* God saturates the Bible with His promises of rewards for obedience to Him.

The most important thing to remember is that our obedience may allow us to reap many blessings on earth, but the best reward of all and the one and only reward that we can truly put stock in through our continued faith is that we will spend eternity with Jesus.

Even if our obedience doesn't reap worldly rewards, we can look forward to reaping our eternal reward—heaven! Matthew 5:12 says, *"Rejoice and be glad, because great is your reward in heaven, for in the same way they persecuted the prophets who were before you."* I came to understand through this verse in Matthew that my obedience could not be dependent on whether or not people agreed with me. Consider the ridicule that Noah must have endured while building the ark. Surely the people viciously harassed him for building an ark, but Noah continued to strive towards pleasing God and not man. Noah put God first.

At this time in my life, my heart was changed, my hunger for the Word was being satisfied, my thirst for God's involvement in my life was quenched and I was finally willing to follow. In my pursuit to be obedient in trying to pursue God's will, I reluctantly registered to attend a Proverbs 31 Christian speakers/writers conference taking place in August of 2005. This weekend turned out to be not just a conference to learn about speaking and writing, as I had anticipated, but instead it turned out to be a an absolutely wonderful spiritual revival, which empowered me to move forward with my calling and allow God to begin using me to make a difference in His kingdom.

Although God is invisible, I clearly saw Him that weekend, in body and spirit. I encountered God with every ounce of my heart, mind and soul. I saw Him actively work in the lives of hundreds of women who had attended the conference and His presence filled the air. This weekend of spiritual renewal had my heart on fire for God, but there was just one problem—I was scheduled to meet with two publishers that weekend about publishing this book.

The whole weekend had been so wonderful and spiritually empowering, but now the dreadful time had come, that I would actually have to sit in front of someone and tell him or her about my past. It was no longer just words on paper held privately and securely on my computer. I was actually going to be confronted with sitting in front of another person and speaking the word "abortion" out loud. The insecurities and fears of judgment came flooding down on me like tidal wave over a small fragile village. By now, I was really getting tired of gasping for air in all these floods in my life! At least Noah's flood only lasted 40 days and nights! But as I tried to mentally prepare to meet with the publishers, I was suddenly weak with fear and dread and seriously regretted my decision to meet with them. Oh, how I wished I had not scheduled those appointments— what had I been thinking!? But since I had committed to meet with them and they were expecting me, it was too late to back out.

As I know so well now, God's love and reassurance is never-ending. He wants to be our security blanket, just like a baby who needs her blanket to feel safe in her crib. I went to the first appointment and sat nervously in the chair in front of the first publisher, wishing I actually had a blanket to cover my face with.

My heart was pounding. My face was probably as white as a sheet. Then I heard her say the words I had been dreading, "So, tell me what your book is about." I choked back the tears and the embarrassment and very briefly told her what the book was about. After speaking, I am confident that I portrayed the "deer in headlights" look. I even felt like one, as if I was standing in the middle of the dark road waiting to be crushed by a huge, fast-moving vehicle, as I awaited her reaction.

Time seemed to stand still and I not only felt like a frozen deer, but one that was toppling on the edge of a cliff waiting for a gust of wind to knock my feet out from under me so I could plunge to a fiery hell. But as only God could plan it, this Godly woman revealed to me that she too had an abortion when she was young and she rejoiced with me in my willingness to want to witness to others through my struggles. She did not judge me or look at me with disgust, but instead she showered me with compassion, understanding and encouragement. She understood my brokenness and my regret.

Now what is the likelihood of that happening? Probably slim to none! I know we should expect the unexpected from God, but when something this miraculous occurs and you know only God could have so divinely and perfectly arranged it, it is so powerful. I survived that meeting and left that room feeling overwhelmed with the mercy that God had just shown me.

A few hours later, the time came to meet with the second publisher. Even though the first appointment had gone very well and I was profoundly thankful for God's intervention and mercy, I wasn't sure if I could talk about the topic of the book again. I hadn't acknowledged my horrendous mistake to anyone in almost 20 years and now I was forced to do it twice in one day!

The second publisher was a very warm and inviting woman, until she said the dreaded words… "So, tell me what your book is about." The minute I opened my mouth, the tears started pouring! The flood was not only in my mind now—it was all over my face! I had tried so hard to be strong and courageous. I had prayed for God to help me control my emotions, but the minute I opened my mouth, the flood began! Apparently all the emotions that I had harbored inside all day and for many, many years, just burst forth like a tidal wave. But my loving God wasn't going to let me down after all this and I should have remembered that He was in control. This wonderful lady comforted me and understood my pain and she spoke words of encouragement. She told me that she "celebrated" with me, because she knew how hard this must be for me, but how proud she was that someone would take a stand for Christ and be willing to share their testimony of pain, suffering and triumph. Someone was celebrating with me! Those words just stuck in my heart! She *celebrated* with me!

After those two meetings, I had to fall on my face and once again, as a little child hanging her head low in shame or a dog retreating with his tail in between his legs, ask God for forgiveness for not having more faith in Him. After all He had done for me, I should have known that He would be in control of any situation that He leads me into. I thought about all the miracles that I had witnessed over the past few years, just as Moses had done, but still I had lacked faith. Even though those two appointments didn't result in my book getting published, it was a huge step of faith that allowed me to move my journey to the next level.

Later that evening at our conference dinner, after a powerful sharing of faith and testimony, each woman was asked to put their burdens, or lies that Satan tells them about themselves, onto a postcard and nail it to a cross. There were two wooden crosses at the front of the room, waiting for our sins to be nailed to them. The symbolism of this act was awesome and almost indescribable. After much procrastination, which I am obviously known for, I hesitantly wrote down the lie that Satan had been telling me for years. My fingers felt like sticks and I had to force myself to scribble the words. But when I was finished, my postcard simply read, *"God would never forgive me for my abortion."* There it was, Satan's lie, in black and white for all to see.

I hid my note card in my pocket and slowly made my way to the front of the room and waited my turn in line at the cross. As I heard the sound of the hammers pounding the nails into the crosses, as I listened to women weeping, knowing that they had given their burdens to God, possibly for the first time, the tears started streaming. God was there with us in that room and His angels were hovering over us so loudly that you could almost hear the flutter of their wings.

I stood in front of the cross, which was now covered in white from all the cards that had been nailed to it. I reached down and picked up a nail and then picked up the hammer with my quivering hands. I put my card on the cross, hoping that no one behind me would see what I had written on my card and I pounded the hammer onto that nail, over and over again until it was securely affixed to the cross. I had literally, physically, nailed my sin to the cross of my savior. The thought that Jesus had been nailed to that cross so that I could be forgiven of that sin would break even the hardest of hearts. Life is hard, but we don't have to get hard with it. I knew that this symbolic act of nailing these burdens to the cross would soften up my heart in a way that I had never allowed it to soften before and shatter the anger and bitterness that had been holding my heart hostage for years. A few years earlier I had accepted God's forgiveness, but now I had actually nailed that burden to the cross and it was no longer mine.

I turned to return to my seat, looking the same on the outside but forever changed on the inside. But this time, the change was positive—I was no longer broken and headed for destruction; instead I was healed and headed for glory. Like only a loving father could do, I could feel my Lord's huge hands wrapped around my heart once again.

Before the participants in the session had begun the process of nailing their burdens to that cross, we had been told that after doing that we should select a Bible verse from a basket full of verses; the speaker had prayed that God would lead each person's hand to the exact verse they needed to hear. So as I turned to return to my seat, burden-free, I reached over and pulled out a little slip of paper, wondering what God was going to say to me.

The verse that God so divinely guided my fingers to was Isaiah 43:18-19: *"Forget the former things; do not dwell on the past. See, I am doing a new thing! Now it springs up; do you not perceive it? I am making a way in the desert and streams in the wasteland."*

Thank you Lord. I do understand. And I promise, cross my heart, that I WILL OBEY.

TWELVE
The "Arc" Lands on the Rock

*Genesis 8:13: "...Noah then removed the covering from the
ark and saw that the surface of the ground was dry. By the
twenty-seventh day of the second month the earth was
completely dry. Then God said to Noah, "Come out of the
ark, you and your wife and your sons and wives."*

Indigo—The Magnificent Color of Royalty

I had left the speakers/writers' conference a changed woman. I now knew, without a shadow of a doubt, that I was truly a member of the royal family—the family of the King of all Kings, Jesus Christ. I was a daughter of the Most High King! I knew I was worthy to wear the purple robes of our Lord; after all, I was His child! I was a princess of spiritual royalty! I was ready to open the doors of my ark, where I had been held captive all these years, and run towards the arcs of my rainbow!

I continued to search God's word for guidance about my journey, as my excitement and enthusiasm was building day by day. I began to envision the pot of gold at the end of my rainbow. My rainbow was now filled with wonderful and beautiful colors. I was overflowing with excitement and anticipation to discover what God had in store for me. One day in my quiet time, I was reminded of the familiar story of the loaves and fishes in the book of Matthew.

Despite his grief over the death of John the Baptist, Jesus spent his afternoon healing the sick, witnessing to crowds of people and sharing the words of His Heavenly Father. The disciples suggested to Jesus that he send the crowd away, as it was time for dinner. Jesus quickly replied that they did not need to go away. Matthew 14:17-21: " *'We have here only five loaves of bread and two fish,' they answered. 'Bring them here to me,' he said. And he directed the people to sit down on the grass. Taking the five loaves and the two fish and looking up to heaven, he gave thanks and broke the loaves. Then he gave them to the disciples and the disciples gave them to the people. They all ate and were satisfied and the disciples picked up twelve basketfuls of broken pieces that were left over. The number of those who ate was about five thousand men, besides women and children.* "

Jesus took something small, insignificant and incapable of meeting the needs of those around Him and transformed it into a method of meeting the needs of thousands of men, women and children.

For many years, behind the smile on my face, I had felt small, insignificant, unworthy and incapable of meeting anyone's needs. I wasn't a good enough wife, mother, sister, daughter, daughter-in-law, friend, employee or boss. I wasn't worthy of God's forgiveness. I wasn't worthy of His love. I wasn't worthy of His grace and mercy. I wasn't worthy of the incredible blessings that had already been bestowed upon me despite my sin and lack of faith. Or was I?

For the first time in my life, I could answer that question with a resounding "Yes!" I was worthy, but not because of anything I had done on my own, good or bad, but only because God sent His one and only Son to die on the cross for my sins, so that I could spend eternity with him. I was worthy and I was finally cleansed and whole.

I carried this newfound freedom and wholeness in my heart each day and tried to continue to live out my life in a way that would glorify

God. However, the personal strain and emotional drain of my corporate job continued to worsen and although I tried to keep my little light shining, the devil was making every effort to snuff it out.

It seemed that the harder I tried, the harder things became. No matter how hard I worked, it was never enough. No matter how much I tried to succeed, the less I seemed to accomplish. The new expectations that were being placed on me by my superiors seemed to be out of my reach. Despite my continued efforts to please my supervisors and my desires to be a good boss and employee, problems continued to abound from every direction. It was as if a black cloud was following me around at work like the one you see over Linus's head in the Charlie Brown cartoons. I began feeling very hopeless about this work situation, but also felt totally defenseless to change it.

In October of 2004, after a harshly critical and rather grueling performance review, despite my love for the Lord and belief in my worthiness in His eyes, I was feeling completely worthless again in the eyes of the world. Although I knew in my heart that much of the criticism bestowed upon me at the hands of this non-Christian man was untrue, biased, vindictive and unprofessional, my self-confidence was at an all-time low. I had come to feel so unneeded, so unimportant, so beaten down and so, so replaceable. It's simply amazing what rejection and heartless criticism can do to a woman's heart.

As a result, I had become stressed, irritable, resentful and unhappy, which began to overlap into my personal life and only heightened my feelings of unworthiness as a mom, a wife and a woman. It had become painfully clear that I was not where God wanted me to be. Although I should not have allowed one person to make me feel so worthless, I knew that this was definitely not the unfathomable blessings that I had hoped for when I promised God I would obey His will. But actions speak louder than words and it was high time for some action. If I wanted to see some action from God, I needed to give God some action!

On November 1, 2004, I found myself crying big crocodile tears as I endured the dreadful, one-hour rush-hour commute to work and anticipated another stressful, unrewarding and draining day. It had come to the point where I started out each day with a nervous stomach, a headache and absolutely no joy.

I pleaded to God and cried out for his mercy. As if God wasn't already aware, I described in great detail to Him about how unhappy I had become with this "dream job," how tired I was of being treated as if I had no feelings, and how utterly saddened I was with the lack of evidence of Christ in my work environment. I just could not operate in the same thoughtless and conniving ways that the corporate world often wanted me to operate by, and as a result I seemed to be the one getting thrown out in the cold. Office politics can really take a toll on the heart of a woman. Therefore, I determined it was the perfect time to let God know about all the problems and injustices that were being bestowed upon me. Just last year, things seemed to be going great at work and I was on top of the world, but now it had become a drain on my life, sucking the joy out of my every breath. I informed God that I was at my wit's end and that I knew I needed to make a change. But what? And how? And when?

I just didn't think that my husband and I could survive financially without my income. Plus I had worked hard to get where I was and I was in a position of authority, seniority and respect. How could I sacrifice all of that and my salary, despite my sheer unhappiness?

I ended my prayer by asking God to show me the way and let me know what my next step should be. I pleaded for Him to make it clear to me about what I should do. I made sure he understood how badly I wanted to be able to resign from the stress of the corporate world and be a stay-at-home mom so that I could devote my life to caring for my three little angels, but deep down in my heart I still harbored the desire to be a professional career woman. I was confused and hopeless. I was truly, honestly, completely broken. Once again, my brokenness and vulnerability opened the doors for God to enter my heart and prepared my ears to hear His voice. When we have lost all hope and our only other recourse it to surrender it all over to God, only then can He truly use us and work through us. If you are feeling broken, then you are ready for God to speak. Are you listening to Him?

Psalms 35: 17-18 tells us this, *"The righteous cry out and the Lord hears them; he delivers them from all their troubles. The Lord is close to the brokenhearted and saves those who are crushed in spirit. "* Despite what we are dealing with, the Lord is there for us, patiently waiting on us to call out to him. Now give him the privilege of listening to you.

Soon after ending my pity party in the car (I had become a master party planner by this time!), I arrived in the parking deck of my office building and was forced to regain my composure, dry my tears, reapply some makeup and load up on the Visine. I trudged into work, downhearted and discouraged, walked to my office and sat down in my important executive chair. I slowly began to carry out my normal morning routine, grabbed a Coke, turned on the computer, opened my inbox and began reading my influx of emails.

As had been the case for several years, my daily Proverbs 31 devotional greeted my eyes at the top of my inbox. Just as I did every morning, I began to read through the devotional, hoping to glean some encouragement to carry me through the day, but not expecting yet another holy encounter. As I read the words on my screen, my heart skipped a beat, my mouth fell open and the blood drained from my tear-stained face. So what was this devotion about, you ask? I want you to read an excerpt from that devotion, written by Glynnis Whitwer, senior editor of the *P31 Woman Magazine* and P31 Speaker:

It was a warm autumn night as I watched my sons practice football. Three other mothers and I lounged in our chairs, alternately glancing at the practice to make sure we saw the tackles and passes and discussing the frustration of preparing dinner on busy weeknights.

As we talked a bit more, I discovered that all three of them worked full-time outside their homes. These devoted moms really wanted to prepare nutritious meals, but it was all they could do to race home from work, grab a quick snack and then race to practice. After practice, they returned home exhausted and grabbed another snack item.

When the conversation turned to me, I shared that because I work part-time from home I was able to make an early dinner. After that, each lady expressed her desire to be home during the day and in almost the same breath, declared why she couldn't do it. My heart broke with compassion because I saw the sense of helplessness in their words and facial expressions. It was as if they were resigned to a full-time job and that was that.

My three football-practice friends are like hundreds of thousands of women across the country who wish they could stay home but don't think it's possible. All they see is one obstacle after another. They see a mountain of debt, the problem of health insurance, a child's empty college fund, an unsupportive spouse or a workplace that "needs" them.

What these women don't see is a God who can handle all those obstacles. Instead of trusting God to provide, they work harder and longer to make ends meet. But the ends just get farther apart.

Psalm 20:7 says, "Some trust in chariots and some in horses, but we trust in the name of the LORD our God." Although that was written thousands of years ago, I wonder if we sometimes

underestimate God's capabilities and trust in our own "horses"
and "chariots." We may have a head-knowledge about trusting
God, but in reality, we trust in a company, our physical strength,
or our intelligence.

  I've found that sometimes God waits for us to make the first
move, believing that He will take care of us ... Is God asking you
to trust Him today? Is He saying to you, "I've heard your cries;
I know you want to be home. It's now time for you to move on
and make it happen."

I sat at my desk literally stunned, with the tears once again
streaming down my face. Those last few sentences seemed to be in
3-D and had protruded right into my heart! Wow! God had sent me
an email! I was elated at the thought of knowing that He had heard
my cries. Although I had a successful career, He knew my innermost
desire was to be home; His desire was for me to be the best mommy
that I could be. His desire was for me to put Him first, not my job.
But was I ready to make a move? Was I ready to make it happen?
Was I willing to trust in Him and believe that He would take care of
my family if I resigned?

I did believe with all my heart that God was in control and I could
hardly recover from receiving an email from the heavens, but logic
and fear won out over wisdom and faith and I continued to work for
several more months, all the while getting more and more miserable,
spending even more time traveling on business trips, and in turn
continuing to make my husband and children suffer, in addition to my
fragile emotional state of mind.

In fact, I continued to work until I was informed by my supervisor
that I would have to change my work hours, which would result in
being away from my family more and putting even more strain on my
already overloaded life. To say the least, I was infuriated and scared.
I just knew that this was a vindictive attempt to force me to quit. This
was so unfair! How could my employer do this to me? I had given

them the last seven years of my life! I did not deserve to be treated this way! How could God let this happen to me? But after a few weeks of analyzing the situation, I finally realized...what a blessing in disguise! But the true blessing was that when I told my husband about this new requirement. His immediate response was, "We are not doing that, our children come first and we will work it out."

I guess that when God realized that I was having trouble making the first move on my own, He just decided to give me a little push. After much discussion and financial number crunching, my husband and I decided that my working more hours in the office was definitely not in the best interest of our family and we knew that I wanted to pursue my calling as a mother and focus on women's ministry, thus we made the scary decision for me to resign. Regardless of the financial fears that we both felt, we knew it was the right thing to do and we had faith that God would provide. We were at a very important crossroad for our future, but through prayer, Michael's loving support and his financial expertise, we chose to turn down the untrodden road to begin a new chapter for our family. We knew we would have to make sacrifices and I would most certainly need to register myself in a shopper's anonymous group very quickly, but in our hearts we couldn't wait to begin the new journey that God had nudged us into.

Although there were circumstances at my place of employment that were very difficult and hurtful and I was glad that I was being given the opportunity to leave the corporate setting, I still had some regrets. I had made some wonderful and dear friends of whom I cherished; I had been employed by that organization for seven years and it was a part of my life; I had worked my way up the corporate ladder; there were certain aspects in my job that I did enjoy and that made me feel successful and challenged; this career was my comfort zone. Oops—therein lay the problem. God will always find a way to get us out of our comfort zone if His desire is for us to follow Him instead. What once had been a great job had become a miserable way to spend my days. I now understand that God will get his point across one way or another, even if it takes pushing us to the breaking point to get our attention. His plans are not our plans.

Needless to say, despite my desire to be at home and to get out under from the cloud of despair that I had been living in, it was a really hard decision to make. But I was broken, I recognized that I was broken and I was ready to be healed and live a life of joy instead of burden. I had to admit to myself that the disadvantages of this job far outweighed the advantages and those few advantages didn't hold a candle to the joy that God had in store for me. Psalms 35:14 says: *"The Lord is close to the brokenhearted and saves those who are crushed in spirit."* Was I brokenhearted? Had my spirit been crushed? Was God close to me and reaching out to save me? Absolutely!

As only God could have planned it, the weekend prior to my submitting my resignation was the weekend of the Proverbs 31 speakers/writers' conference, which I have already told you about, and as a result, my faith and love for the Lord was at an all time high! The burning spiritual passion in my heart helped me to have the confidence and wisdom to know that I was making the right move by leaving my comfort zone…the move that God had been waiting so patiently for me to make.

Ten short (but miserable) months since God had sent me an email confirming that He desired for me to be home, I had a brand new important job title, "stay-at-home mom," and a brand new boss, God himself. Within ten months of hearing God's voice loud and clear and even seeing it in black and white via modern technology, my dream had come true! Although we had lost my entire salary, God provided for all of our financial needs in a variety of blessed and miraculous ways.

I have heard many personal testimonies in which a person testifies that God had been calling them for a long period of time, even years, to serve Him or work in a particular ministry, but they refused to listen or were too scared to step out of their comfort zone. I always thought that made for a great testimony, but never truly understood how God could have been speaking to someone and calling him or her to a purpose, of which they willfully refused. How dare they not listen to God like that? But, we all live and learn, and now I can attest to that same statement.

Is it possible that God has been calling you and you have politely, but adamantly, declined? If you think that he has been calling you, or you know he has been calling you, but you are hesitant to answer, I want to encourage you to be open to listening and open to following. Don't waste as much time as I wasted trying to take care of things on my own and allowing fear to take my heart hostage. Be open to making that first move and allow God to take care of you!

In the book titled *What Happens When Women Walk in Faith*, Lysa TerKeurst says this: "Our thoughts about how God wants to use us are much too small. If we could taste the delights that await us in the promised land, we'd leave everything behind without hesitation...and yet God doesn't work that way. We must choose to leave first. We must see by faith the rewards ahead and then move toward them."

When our eyes are finally opened and we can see God's will and the plan that He so divinely put in place, it is nothing less than astonishing, breathtaking and powerful. Looking back and seeing how God planned my life, from the moment of conception in my mother's womb to the present day, literally brings me to my knees in amazement and praise for His almighty power.

My life's journey began in January 1967, when I was born into a loving Christian family. January was the month that my first child would have been born, had I chosen to give him or her life. January is "ironically" national Sanctity of Life month, which I was forced to acknowledge every year in church as I watched videotapes about the horror of abortion and the importance of pro-life and as I simultaneously mourned the anniversary of my lost child and longed for them to be in my life.

January 1994 is the month that my first precious little angel was born into our family. In fact, she was born on January 22—the exact anniversary date of the *Roe v. Wade* court decision to legalize abortion. I think it's time to acknowledge that irony is a horrendous myth! Every big and little thing that happens in this world is God-ordained!

January is obviously a month that holds great meaning in my life. It is a month that signifies life, death, rebirth and new birth. Only God could have created such an awesome and symbolic pattern in my life. Can you now see that God's plans are not our plans? His plans are put into being before we are even born, but He patiently and lovingly allows us time to figure out what His plans are.

Also consider this spiritual "irony"—my mother named me Tracie, which means "battler or courageous warrior." My middle name is Renee, which by some interpretations means, "peace or grace." Although my mother thought she was choosing my birth name merely because she favored it, God also had His hand in the name game. He knew that one day I would need to be courageous to overcome the obstacles that would take place in my life; He knew I would one day become a warrior in the battle to build his kingdom and defend His name; and most importantly, He also knew I would need a lot of His grace and peace to pull through!

God has been calling me for many years. He birthed me into a Christian family. He began calling me ever so gently on that sorrowful summer night in 1986 when I lay in my bed crying, but I was too grief-stricken to listen. God was calling me during my college years as I gradually wandered into the wilderness, but I was too busy enjoying my independence and having fun. God was calling me in the first few years of my marriage, but I was too focused on handling things on my own. God was calling me after my three wonderful children were born, but I was too busy building a career and raising my family.

Fortunately, our heavenly Father does not give up on His children. He persevered and continued to call out to me, despite my obvious negligence to listen and then my obvious and determined unwillingness to obey. But He never gave up on me. Even after years of wandering alone without His hand in mine, He called me to a church home. He called me to attend Bible studies for the first time in my life. He called me to attend the Proverbs 31 seminar. He guided my hands to pick out books that would minister to my exact needs. He called me to the Beth Moore conference. He called me to spend time in His Word. He called me to begin a women's ministry newsletter to reach out to others in faith and use my gift of writing for writing devotions to encourage others. He called me to submit my marriage to Him and be willing to be submissive to my husband. He called me to get involved with women's ministry. He called me to be a stay-at-home mom. He called me to write a book. He called me to become a speaker and share my testimony with groups of women whose lives could be changed through hearing my testimony and God's story. He called me to be used as a tool to bring glory to his kingdom. He called me to help light the way for other people to leave the dark shadows of sin and discover His light, the light to make rainbows glimmer. He called me to be a soldier in His mighty spiritual army—a soldier that is no more important than any of the soldiers in God's army, but also no less important either. He called me to fulfill His plan. He called me to obey. God had been calling me for nearly 20 years and I was finally ready to listen and ready to submit my life to Him.

Now I am truly able to understand the meaning of Matthew 16: 24-25, *"Then Jesus said to his disciples, 'If anyone would come after me, he must deny himself and take up his cross and follow me. For whoever wants to save his life will lose it, but whoever loses his life for me will find it.'"* I was saved by His grace and blessed by His mercy. In order to have a life of glory, I had to lay down my pride and my shame, my job and my entire life, and give my life fully to Him. Only then could I be rewarded with a new life that only He could provide. God was resurrecting and recreating me. Thank goodness God specializes in resurrections!

I am not qualified or worthy to be used by God. Nothing I have ever done, nor will I ever do, will make me a worthy or viable instrument in God's orchestra of life. Ephesians 2:8 tells us: *"For it is by grace you have been saved, through faith—and this not from yourselves, it is the gift of God—not by works, so that no one can boast."* But He continued to call me over a process of many years—many years in which He should have grown weary of my disobedience. God did not call me because I was qualified to serve Him. He called me to pay attention to Him so that He could qualify me to serve, and He spent nearly 20 years preparing me for that service. And somewhere along the journey, His preparation led me to His peace and now I believe that God can use any circumstance for His glory. My ability to finally acknowledge that has allowed my heart to heal in a way that it could have never healed on its own.

Each arc of color of my rainbow is finally formed. Most importantly, the arc of my rainbow had landed firmly on the rock…the Rock of Salvation, that is. My "ark" was now securely affixed on the Rock of Salvation, through the beautiful "arcs" of my colorful rainbow. I now had the wisdom to rely on Psalm 18:2: *"The Lord is my rock, my fortress and my deliverer."*

Also consider this verse in Psalm 40:2: *"He lifted me out of the slimy pit, out of the mud and mire, he set my feet on a rock and gave me a firm place to stand."* That slimy pit that I had been in was merely a faint memory now! My feet were on the rock and I was standing firm…finally! I am bursting with excitement and anticipation to see where God is going to lead me, and to see the mystery unfold as to what God desires to do through me for His kingdom.

Ephesians 3:20 says: *"Now to him who is able to do immeasurably more than all we ask or imagine, according to his power that is at work within us…"* What an encouragement this verse is to those who are willing to follow Jesus and pursue His will. This verse tells us that we should expect great things to happen in our lives and through our lives, but not by our own power or works, but only through the awesome and supernatural power of the Holy Spirit. When we accept that His power lives within us, only then can we accomplish things that are beyond our wildest dreams. Through this holy power, we can do things that we never thought we were capable of doing. We can have a part in transforming other people's lives, as God uses us as his instrument for transformation. What an honor it is to be used by God!

God's calling began long before I was born, for He knew the plans he had for me. Jeremiah 1:5 says: *"Before I formed you in the womb, I knew you, before you were born I set you apart; I appointed you as a prophet to the nations."* Before I was in my mother's womb, He knew the foundational faith that my parents would instill in me. He selected the perfect month for me to draw my first breath. He knew what sins I would commit at the fragile age of 19. He knew that I would one day be a lost sheep, but that I would eventually be reunited with my shepherd. He knew the plans He had for me in His kingdom as a result of being lost. God did not "choose" me because I sinned and triumphed, instead He gave me the opportunity to serve Him as part of the infinite plan that He put in place long before I was in existence. All I had to do was simply say, "Yes, Lord, I will follow you."

Is there something you need to say yes to today? If so, or if you are unsure, stop right now where you are and pray fervently for God to speak to you and make His will known to you. Or if you know His will already but have been hesitant to obey Him, say "Yes" right now!

Consider this verse once more, in Ephesians 3:20: *"Now to him who is able to do immeasurably more than all we ask or imagine, according to his power that is a work within us."* Dear sister in Christ, believe and it will happen.

My only regret now is that I hadn't obeyed God's command earlier and that I wasted so many years in disobedience due to my own human fears. But I know I am forgiven for that delay to obey as well and I have to focus on the future that God has set before me. I can now focus on the truth that I am finally free! The heavy chains and gripping handcuffs that I had allowed Satan to keep me in bondage with for so many years have disintegrated and fallen to the ground in pieces. They can never restrain me from praising my Lord ever again.

Even though my rainbow exists only in my heart, I know that it is so bright now that if it were to shine in the sky for all to see, one could barely view it without shielded eyes. The quantity of colors, the quality of all the bright colors and the thousands of colors all mixed together, would make for a glorious sight. The only thing that could possibly cast a shadow on me now is the gentle shadow of angel's wings as they hover over me singing God's praises.

My life is a masterpiece that the all-powerful God has painted with His loving and attentive hands. Luckily, it is a masterpiece that will never be finished until I leave this world to spend eternity with Him. Each day of my life I discover new colors in my rainbow and new paragraphs to add to my story. Our story is forever being written, until we reach the heavenly gates and God is the ultimate author.

Everyone knows that the pot of gold at the end of the rainbow is just a myth and there really aren't any little green men running around in tights trying to protect their precious treasure. But as children of God, we can live confidently knowing that when we reach the end of our rainbow, we will find a treasure—the treasure of salvation! We can look forward to an eternity in heaven with the holy trinity as the pot of gold at the end of our rainbow of life.

Noah obeyed God. He didn't understand what God had planned, but he knew he needed to obey. Obeying God meant that Noah had to endure unending criticism and harsh judgment by those around him, but he persevered with God's command. He was forced to spend more than 40 days and nights on a crowded boat with a lot of smelly animals who probably would have liked to eat him for dinner. He had to dwell in close quarters with his entire family and was never able to get away from them! He endured hardships and pain. But as a result of his faith, obedience and commitment, God saved Noah, physically, spiritually and eternally. God saved and blessed Noah's family. Noah and his family reaped the blessings of his obedience and at the end of his journey, he was the first person to peer out the window of the ark and see the very first vibrant, colorful rainbow perfectly formed and splashed against the blue sky in a glowing and beautiful masterpiece that only the God of the heavens and earth could have painted. I can only imagine how his eyes surely swelled with tears and his heart pounded with joy at the sight of such a magnificent array of beauty.

When we devote our lives to Christ and make every effort to live a life that will bring glory to Him, even though we will stumble many, many, many times along the way, God will give us much more than a pot of gold. Instead, when we reach the end of our rainbow, we will find streets of gold, and those streets will lead to an eternity of happiness, love and fulfillment with our Lord Jesus Christ.

THIRTEEN
Building Your Own Rainbow

Do you know what God's plan is for your life? Have you heard Him calling you, but been hesitant to answer?

Your calling may be to minister to little children as a choir or Sunday school teacher; to feed the hungry in your community; to reach out to those dealing with the loss of loved ones; to provide coats to children who have no heat during the frigid winter months; to travel to another country for a missions project; to help plan beautiful weddings; to be a Godly role model for your husband and children; to be a witness to people in your workplace; to plan and teach Bible studies to help your neighbors come to know Christ; to show love and understanding to women who have suffered through a divorce; to provide a backyard Bible school to help children know about Jesus; to be a Christian speaker; to become a minister; or to work with crisis pregnancy centers and counsel and love women who had abortions. Maybe your calling does not require huge sacrifice, embarrassment or shame, or maybe it does, but, dear one, whatever it is, please say YES. Don't waste time, just obey.

In Joel Osteen's book, titled *Living Your Best Life Now*, he encourages us to expect more from God than what we think is impossible with our human minds. Joel says, "Raise your level of expectancy. It's our faith that activates the power of God. Let's quit limiting Him with our small-minded thinking and start believing Him for bigger and better things. Remember, if you obey God and are willing to trust Him, you will have the best this life has to offer—and more! Make a decision that from this day forward, you are going to be excited about the life God has for you."

God has so many things already planned for you. Get excited about it! God wants to give you His favor, he is just waiting for you to ask so that He can rain that favor upon you! He has so many vibrant shades of beautiful colors that He wants to fill your life with, if only you will trust and obey. Remember the old hymn? The lyrics say "Trust and obey, for there's no other way to be happy in Jesus, than to trust and obey." Are you willing to let him begin building your bridge to freedom and creating your magnificent rainbow? Then trust and obey!

Regardless of what your unique calling may be, I want to encourage you to set out on a wonderful journey today to discover it. Trust in God's word and have faith that God has a plan for you. His plan was put in place when you settled into your mother's womb and He has a divine purpose for your life and desires to use YOU to build His kingdom.

If you are having difficulty seeing God's purpose for your life, call out to him and ask His forgiveness for any unconfessed sins. If you feel you may have an unconfessed sin which is putting up a wall between you and God, then take a moment to confess that sin. Matthew 7:7-8 says: *"Ask and it will be given to you; seek and you will find; knock and the door will be opened to you. For everyone who asks receives; he who seeks finds; and to him who knocks, the door will be opened."* So what are you waiting for? Ask God to open your eyes, ask him for blessings, ask Him for guidance, ask Him for compassion, ask Him for forgiveness and ask Him for healing and renewal. Ask Him to give you a hunger and thirst for Him that consumes your every thought. Believe me, believe God, you will receive!

Be assured that God hears your prayers and He forgives you. That only leaves one last task—you have to forgive yourself for the sins that burden your heart. If you have asked for God's saving forgiveness and grace, but have never had the strength to forgive yourself for your past mistakes, please pray this prayer:

Most heavenly Father, you know I have sinned and I confess this sin to you. I ask for your forgiveness, your mercy, your grace. I also ask forgiveness for not making you a priority in my life and for not being willing to accept your forgiveness in the past. Please help me to forgive myself and to realize that I am worthy of your love and the mercy and grace that you will bestow upon me. I am worthy to serve you. I praise you for who you are and for what you have done in my life. Please be with me Lord and make your presence known to me. Open my eyes to hear your voice and help me to see your will for my life with full clarity. In Jesus' name, Amen.

If you are not a Christian, or are unsure of your salvation, this is a perfect opportunity to accept Christ into your heart, or to ask him into your life again. You have almost completed reading this book and have witnessed how actively God worked in my life. My story is no different than that of millions of Christians since the beginning of time. God is alive and active! He wants to work in your life too!

All you have to do to harvest his supernatural intervention and power in your life is to accept Him. I pray that if you are reading this book because you were looking for an answer to your questions about sin and forgiveness and seeking to find out if God really does love you, that you will walk away from this book with an overwhelming understanding and acceptance that God loves you. He has been waiting on you to come to Him. Now is the time to enter into His presence. I want you to close your eyes and envision Jesus standing at your door, peering at you through the glass, arms stretched out wide and waiting eagerly for you to open your door and fall into His arms.

If you are ready to accept Him, if your heart has a void in it that you have tried to fill with everything else but God, if you continue to feel unworthy and incapable of being all you can be, if you continue to feel an emptiness in your heart, please take a moment right now to pray the simple sinner's prayer: *"Lord, I accept you as my Lord. I now understand that you are truly the King of all kings. I am a sinner and I seek your forgiveness for my sins. Thank you for sending your son to die on the cross for me so that I could spend eternity in heaven with you. I accept that you are the one and only savior and that you always have been and always will be. I love you, Lord. Amen."*

Blessed child, you have now entered the kingdom of God. Welcome.

If you are unsure of what your calling is, please seek God's face, be in constant prayer and ask God to make His will known to you. God might send you an email, or speak to you in another way that He knows will catch your attention! But rest assured, He will make His will known, if only you ask. So be ready for an answer! Don't brush off things that seem a little ironic or circumstantial, for that could be your heavenly answer! God deals in truth, not irony! He is patiently waiting for an open ear and a willing heart and He is bursting at the seams to have a conversation with you! Yes, you!

If your life seems to be in complete disarray right now and nothing is going right; if hardships seem to be looming around every corner; if your pain and suffering seem never-ending; if all seems hopeless— then you are ready. You are broken. You are vulnerable. You are right where God needs you to be. Now is the time—invite God in— and let Him work His miracles in your life. Give him a chance to redeem you. Don't blame Him—love Him. He loves you regardless of whether or not you accept His love, but He is waiting for you.

I came across a poem in a book, which was once written by an unknown author:

What is life?
Life is a gift...accept it
Life is an adventure...dare it
Life is a mystery...unfold it
Life is a game...play it
Life is a struggle...face it
Life is a beauty...praise it
Life is a puzzle...solve it
Life is opportunity...take it
Life is sorrowful...experience it
Life is a song...sing it
Life is a goal...achieve it
Life is a mission...fulfill it

If I could, I would add just one more line to that poem: *Life is a rainbow...discover it!*

Don't doubt for a moment whether or not God is calling you to an ordained plan that He decided for you while you lay in your mother's womb. He is most definitely calling you, even if you have yet to hear His voice. Keep in mind that God does not speak to us like the great and powerful Oz! He is loving, subtle, quiet and gentle. You have to be listening in order to hear. And if you are listening and you are ready and willing to fulfill a purpose in this world that no one can fill except for you, He will call you.

God is longing for you, waiting for you to open your spiritual ears and have a conversation with Him. In John and Staci Eldridge's book, *Captivating*, regarding the image of a woman being like that of God, they made this comment, "There is a radiance hidden in your heart that the world desperately needs." The world needs you to shine your light, to share your rainbow, to fulfill your divine purpose. The world needs your voice. You have a purpose in this life. It's time to discover it.

Once God helps you define your purpose through prayer and intervention in your life, don't procrastinate, just go for it! When God opens a door, He not only wants us to walk through that door, He expects and desires for us to walk through it. You will not be able to see the magnitude of what God has planned for your life, until you are willing to take that first step and walk over the threshold to start your own exciting journey.

Who knows, it is highly possible that in your quest for discovery of your calling and throughout the exciting journey to reinvent your own rainbow, you may help someone else to discover his or her rainbow as well.

FOURTEEN
The True Meaning of the Rainbow of Life

Red

Red is for the sins I have committed and the many sins I have yet to commit in my life. Red also represents the suffering that Christ endured when He died on the cross for my sins. Red stands for the blood that Christ shed on my behalf, so that I could be forgiven, renewed and guaranteed eternal life.

Matthews 26:26: *"This is my blood of the covenant, which is poured out for many for the forgiveness of sins…"*

Orange

Orange has a root meaning of "separation." For years I was separated from God, as I allowed sin to build the wall higher and higher between God and the forgiveness that I was so desperate for. But orange also signifies the sweet, fragrant fruits that God wants to bear, through His children and through our obedient service to Him.

Ephesians 5:1-2: *"Be imitators of God, therefore, as dearly loved children and live a life of love, just as Christ loves us and gave himself up for us as a fragrant offering and sacrifice to God."*

Yellow

Yellow is often associated with cowardliness. Yellow represents the fear that I once held in my heart, but which was overcome through the power of our Lord Jesus Christ. Yellow is also the color of the sunshine, which warms the earth with its brightness. Yellow represents God's shining light on the world and is a constant reminder that we are to be a lighthouse for Him. Let your light shine for Jesus!

Psalm 27:1: *"The Lord is my light and my salvation—whom shall I fear?"*

Green

The word "green" often infers immaturity and lack of experience. However, being in the green phase of your rainbow is merely the beginning of a journey. Green is the phase in which we can learn and eventually sprout wings and begin to fly. Green is also the color of the trees and plants and was the color of the Garden of Eden. So ultimately, green is a beautiful symbol of creation, discovery, purpose and happiness.

Psalm 68:3: *"But may the righteous be glad and rejoice before God; may they be happy and joyful."*

Blue

Blue is an easily interpreted color. Blue carries the burden of depression and sadness and is the color we become when we allow our sin to hold us hostage. But blue can also be the color of a beautiful summer sky. It is the heavenly home for all rainbows, big or small. Blue is where the horizon touches the outskirts of heaven. Blue is a vivid reminder of heaven, as we eagerly await the day that Jesus returns to earth as He has promised and whisks us away into eternal happiness.

Isaiah 35:10: *"...and the ransomed of the Lord will return. They will enter Zion with singing, everlasting joy will crown their heads. Gladness and joy will overtake them and sorrow and sighing will flee away."*

Indigo/Violet

The root meaning of indigo is "to cover." We are only human and when we sin, we want to cover it up. We don't want God to see it and we don't want anyone on earth to see it or know about it. But when we are covered with sin, God cannot look upon us. We must repent and at that time, He will reap His blessings upon us, the very moment that we ask Him to forgive us of our sins.

Acts 10:43: *"All the prophets testify about him that everyone who believes in him receives forgiveness of sins through his name."*

Violet is a form of purple, which signifies royalty. Although we don't feel as if we are royal, we are a leader in God's army. Through prayer and petition, we can become one of God's mighty soldiers and symbolically wear the fine linens of royalty that our Lord has bestowed upon us.

Proverbs 31:8: *"She makes coverings for her bed; she is clothed in fine linen and purple."*

Isaiah 14:14: *"I will ascend above the tops of the clouds; I will make myself like the Most High."*

Black

Black is not a color; it is the absence of color. Black signifies the absence of light. Black signifies something being soiled, evil and wicked. Black signifies the absence of God and the absence of love. Even if you think your rainbow is completely black, or has spots of black scattered around within it, it only takes one simple prayer to wash those spots away forever. "Lord, I know I am a sinner. Please forgive me for my many sins. I know that you died on the cross for my sins so I could be saved. Please come into my heart and live forever, until the day that I can join you in heaven for eternity." As soon as that prayer is spoken, your rainbow will begin to appear and your eternal life with Jesus is guaranteed. Nothing can hold back the rainbow once the light has peeked through the darkness. God is the light of the world.

John 3:16: *"For God so loved the world that he gave his one and only Son, that whoever believes in him shall not perish but have eternal life."*

White

White equals purity. Although we can never truly obtain purity because of the reality of sin, we can live a life that strives to achieve it. We can strive for a life that is Christ-like and one that will bless the people around us and bring glory to our Lord.

Isaiah 1:18: *"Come now, let us reason together, says the Lord. Though your sins are like scarlet, they shall be as white as snow, though they are red as crimson, they shall be like wool."*

A goal is just a dream with a deadline. If your goal is to live like Christ, to be a soldier in God's army, to be a lighthouse for Him and allow Him to work through you to make a difference in people's lives, here on earth and for eternity, then I encourage you to pursue it. Keep in mind that it is not merely the achievement of a goal that shows success, but you also get to reap the benefits of building your character by doing everything possible to meet the goal, which in turn will result in you being a more loving, happy, joyful and God-fearing individual. Your only deadline is to establish and meet your goals before it is too late. We only get one chance at life and life is short, so make the best of it today!

Every individual has a different calling or purpose in life, but each and every unique individual most certainly has a calling.

Always remember, that once you get involved with God's dreams, He will get involved with yours.

Tracie Miles is available for speaking engagements, and is a member of the Proverbs 31 Ministries Speaker Team. For more information, please visit www.traciewmiles.com or www.proverbs31.org.